Company Towns of MICHIGAN'S UPPER PENINSULA

I0792587

Christian Holmes

THE History PRESS

Published by The History Press
Charleston, SC 29403
www.historypress.net

Cover images: Delta County Historical Society, Nahma Township Historical Society and Michigan Technological University Archives.

First published 2015

Manufactured in the United States

ISBN 978.1.62619.742.8

Library of Congress Control Number: 2015934850

Dedicated to my father, George, who enjoyed reading the four-volume set of
Michigan as a Province, Territory and State *over and over.*

CONTENTS

PREFACE

This story's journey began in September 2011, when I was invited to a planning meeting for an exhibit at the local Bonifas Art Center in Escanaba. I was enlightened to the prior existence of a company town thirty-five miles from where I had lived for forty years. "The Selling of Nahma" exhibit told the story of the sale of one company town in the Michigan north woods in 1951. My role was to assist in the research, and my investigations led to the discovery of a remarkable number of company towns in Michigan's Upper Peninsula's history, beginning in the 1840s, with some existing into the 1990s. The second "hook" that caught me was that the company town phenomenon received so little mention in the U.P. history literature. Why was this? When The History Press indicated an interest in a telling of the story, I was along for the fascinating ride.

It's impossible to overlook the emotional side of this story. The individuals who lived in these towns experienced remarkable hardships. Working conditions were arduous: logging was done in the winter snow, ice and very low temperatures. The mines were no better—dirty, dangerous work underground by candlelight, with cool stale air and the threat of premature explosion of dynamite or cave-ins. Lumber mill work meant operating mechanical cutting devices before any notion of safety guidelines. Women worked from before sunup to past dusk in cramped conditions. The disparity in wealth with owners could be tolerated only because others' lots were no better. One woman who grew up in the Keweenaw Peninsula had four family members who were either killed or disabled in mine accidents. Lofty talk about acknowledging the interests of investors or owners runs thin in this context.

The next "awakening" I had was in realizing the tremendous debt one has in assembling a story such as this. My confession is that I've too frequently skipped or skimmed the lists of contributors whom authors thank for making their accomplishments possible. My list is long and begins with the scores of historical society volunteers who collect, organize and assemble historical articles, photographs and ephemera to document the history of their communities. Especially notable were the Nahma Township Historical Museum, the IXL Historical Museum, the Delta County Historical Society Archives, the Ontonagon County Historical Museum, the Newton Township Historical Museum and the Chippewa County Historical Society. Notable individuals who assisted from those organizations were Tee Lynts, Glenn Lamberg, Karen Lindquist, Judy Meintz, Joan Daniels, Bernie Arbic, Lucille Kenyon, Daniel Cvengros and Bruce Johanson. The library staff at Bay de Noc Community College, the Escanaba Public Library, Michigan Technological University's Library and Archives, Bayliss Public Library and the J.M Longyear Regional Research Library were also instrumental. Individuals who agreed to be interviewed included Rose Fish, Philip Miller, Albert Winberg and Arne Anderson, among others.

Unique contributions were made by Ann Bissell, Betty Sodders, Sterling McGwinn, CJ Havill, Mary June, William Cummings, Greg Dumais and Ellie O'Donnell. I must also salute the authors listed in the concluding bibliography; they were the trailblazers whose detailed documentation and insight made this overview possible and to whom I owe a tremendous debt. Encouragement and support were provided throughout the three and a half years by my son, Adam; my wife, Linda; and my daughter, Alicia. Heartfelt appreciation to you all.

INTRODUCTION

The common knee-jerk response to the subject of "company towns" is usually negative. We conjure visions of unscrupulous bosses taking unfair advantage of coal miners in West Virginia's Appalachian region, where poor souls never escape a vicious cycle of toil and price gouging as they stumble between deplorable working conditions and the mandatory company store. Tennessee Ernie Ford's ballad line, "I owe my soul to the company store," is etched in the popular subconscious. Historical research presents an opportunity to balance such notions with facts as they emerge.

Much of the Upper Peninsula (U.P.) business history has focused on the industries themselves (e.g., sawmill production and mine equipment) and very little on the lives of those average souls who labored in those firms, let alone the "business model" of the company town. In fact, one could easily conduct a great deal of reading on U.P. business history without any indication that the company town model or some variant of such was common throughout the region. Certainly between 1850 and 1990, there were more industrial locations that did not contain all the hallmarks of a company town (like industry-owned houses and retail stores) than did, but company ownership has not been adequately discussed as a common theme in U.P. history. Over time, the list of such company-funded services expanded from rental housing and retail sales to include medical services, disability payments, pension benefits, construction of community recreation/entertainment centers and free or minimally priced power, water, sewer or wood fuel. These went beyond the extension of a good corporate citizen, such as donating land or building materials for schools or churches.

My research on company towns in the U.P. led to several discoveries on the topic of company towns in general. They have not been confined to the coal mining district of the United States, as examples can easily be found in New England, the South, the West and the Northwest. They are not just a thing of the past or even confined to the United States. Company towns are alive and well in places like Kohler, Wisconsin, and South America, as well as in some of the technology industries. The term "paternalism" is commonly applied to the phenomenon of such company ownership, characterized by single-industry towns where the employer owns a substantial number of employee homes, a "general store" and, frequently, medical services. In the U.P., it was not an "all or nothing" situation with the services. Some employers provided housing but no retail store. In many communities, employees had the option of owning their homes (usually at a distance from the workplace) on either their own land or property rented from the company. Over time, it was not uncommon for tenants to have the option of purchasing their homes. Likewise, many towns had a company store and also a privately owned one, although it was understood that pricing would be comparable.

My interest soon turned to some underlying questions about the phenomenon of company towns, which seem, on the surface, so foreign to our economic and social order in the twenty-first century. Why did they come into existence? Why did this "business model" pass from fashion? How bad were they? And, perhaps, how good were they for the owners? Some of these questions are easier to answer than others. Some will take the duration of this book for the reader to reach a conclusion.

Initially, the company town model was borne out of necessity for many nineteenth-century entrepreneurs and for contemporaries faced with similar obstacles. Provision of housing and other basic living necessities (delivered in a general store) were needed to attract and maintain workers in remote, resource-rich locations. Employers wanted a stable workforce for their mills and mines. Males with families were less apt to leave for greener pastures than their single counterparts. Families required houses, not boardinghouses. Many of these employees were first-generation immigrants who had exhausted their finances to pay for the voyage to this new country. Certainly the character of the company town runs contrary to some of our contemporary values and expressions of personal independence, such as homeownership and unlimited shopping choices. The reader must keep in mind that many of these recent immigrants had left economic and political systems in Europe where political freedom and economic well-being were in the realm of ideals rather than reality.

The motivation for provision of company-financed services changed over time. If employers in undeveloped frontier regions wanted laborers for their ventures, housing and stores were more in the realm of a basic living necessity than an option. Likewise, medical services and the company physician were necessary to deal with industrial accidents. As communities developed in the U.P., the motivation for such services grew more as an antidote to the organized labor development, especially strikes or perceived militancy. Collective bargaining was too great a compromise of the company authority.

The reader must also recognize that in a discussion of company towns in the U.P. (or anywhere), distinctions get blurred. Many sites in the northern peninsula of Michigan were less towns than sparse villages—or, more likely, simply "locations." Also to be considered is that some operations came, thrived and disappeared without being chronicled by recorders or writers. Living descendants of participants or observers are few and far between to tell their stories. In most of the oldest histories, especially related to iron ore mining sites, the focus is almost exclusively on the industrial factors, ignoring the daily living of the employees.

Why did the company town model pass from the modern scene? Some factors were inherent with the model itself. More were related to the changing social and economic environment. As the available supply of natural resources was reduced or depleted, it was time for the company to move on to a new location. As the westward growth in the country continued, so did competition from the western states for copper and timber. Business managers' priorities were really on mining or logging and not on retail store management or landlording/property management. Yes, these were additional revenue streams, but many found them to be a distraction from the focus of their business. The control the company town managers were able to exercise was offset by all the ill will generated from perceptions of bias, favoritism and retail price gouging. At the same time, rent revenue was relatively small, and bad debts from the store had to be absorbed. All of this, of course, has to be considered within the increasing prevalence of trade unionism and second-generation immigrants, whose outlook was more influenced by expression of American values of personal independence than by seeking an alternative to European hard times.

Theories for the phenomenon of change can only truly be tested against historical record. This survey provides a broad scope of company town developments in various Michigan industries in the Upper Peninsula:

copper mines, iron ore mines, lumber mills, limestone quarries and pig iron production. Some accounts are longer than others, based on available information. The sequence is chronological, determined by the arrival of the company. Their stories entertain and expand our perspective on how this region grew into and through the twentieth century.

HOUGHTON AND KEWEENAW COUNTIES

The Keweenaw Peninsula's uniqueness was found not just in its sixty-mile extension north into Lake Superior, its geographically remote location and notorious annual snowfalls but also in the copper on its surface and especially underground. Evidence indicates that prehistoric and Native Americans cleared much of the surface copper. In the 1700s, the first Europeans (French and British) began their exploration and mining. Henry Schoolcraft's early surveying and Douglas Houghton, Michigan's first geologist, verified the nature and distribution of the mineral resources, called "native copper"—90 percent pure and almost unique to the area. Although the Keweenaw Peninsula, or "Copper Country," stretches from its tip ninety miles into Lake Superior, in a southern and western direction to the Ontonagon area, this chapter will focus on the center of the peninsula, specifically on the Calumet/Hancock/Houghton regions. The first mines were located in the 1840s in the northernmost section of the peninsula near Eagle River (Cliffs Mine, National Mine) and the western area near Ontonagon (Minesota Mine). Over the course of the next one hundred years, more than 150 locations were explored, attempted or thrived as viable copper mines. From these, three primary companies emerged and became the major producers and players in the Keweenaw: the Quincy (Hancock area), Calumet and Hecla (originally Red Jacket, name later changed to Calumet) and Copper Range (primarily the area south and west of Houghton).

The opening of the region for mining activity is marked by the 1842 Treaty of La Pointe, when the area was ceded to the federal government by the Native Americans. Adventurous prospectors explored and tested stories from Native Americans and surveyors regarding likely locations for viable mining activities. These prospectors typically sold their discoveries to mining companies, whose investors financed the significant cost of mine equipment and facilities. The region was very undeveloped and dependent on lake travel, especially bringing supplies from the Sault Ste. Marie area and the Detroit/Lake Erie region and, similarly, for returning copper to the industrial and commercial centers to the south and east. This predated the locks at Sault Ste. Marie and the establishment of major railroads, let alone any "highways." Most ventures involved investors from the eastern states (like Massachusetts, Pennsylvania and New York) who bankrolled the startup operations in hopes of lucrative returns on their investments. An excellent illustration of this phenomenon is the title of the classic book *Michigan Copper and Boston Dollars*, by William Gates.

While most company towns in the early years are characterized by little published information, this region's growth, development and community are very well chronicled in excellent books by Alison Hoagland, Larry Lankton, Arthur Thurner and Richard Fields. In what was truly a frontier area, the boardinghouse was frequently one of the first buildings erected for the nearly all-male workforce. The earliest ethnic groups to make the arduous trip were typically the Cornish, who had considerable experience with mining in their homeland of Cornwall, England. They were often followed by the French Canadians and Germans. The mining operations led to two facilities that were linked, but not necessarily at the same location: the mine itself and the mill. The focus at the mine was getting the ore-laden rock out of the ground; the milling entailed the crushing and separating of the ore from the rock with the use of large amounts of water. The latter process led to major accumulations of tailings, discarded ground rock from which much of the copper had been removed. These caused environmental damage, both visually and in soil contamination, but also left an opportunity for later reprocessing for less rich copper content. The mines needed to be where the copper veins or lodes were, and the mills needed access to water, whether Lake Superior or the inland lake, Portage, between Hancock and Houghton. The final player was the smelter, where the copper was melted down into bars or ingots for shipping. The smelters would normally serve several mines and even companies. The final destinations via either water or rail were distant industrial centers for fabrication into copper sheets, tubing, wire and so on.

Simple log cabins followed the boardinghouses (often with as many as seventy beds), as mine officials recognized that married employees were less likely to relocate than single men. These simple cabins, which frequently contained only two rooms on the first floor and an attic, were later eclipsed by increasing complex structures. (The only exception was later when new housing was specifically needed for unskilled laborers.) Initial rents were one dollar per month but gradually increased over time as wages increased and houses improved. A common formula was to charge one dollar per month per room. Improvements in housing over time were made to attract and retain workers and accommodate those in managerial and supervisory positions in the mines, mills and smelters. House foundations evolved from cedar posts to masonry; exterior log walls were replaced with wooden clapboard planks. Windows were added, as were the number of rooms per house and amenities such as porches, halls, mud rooms and plaster and lath interior wall finishing. Only much later did modernization include running water, indoor plumbing and electricity; garbage removal was generally provided by the company.

Company construction and maintenance of homes was almost a universal practice in the Keweenaw, although it should also be noted that such housing represented a fraction of all employee housing. Estimates of the number of company-owned homes in the region range from 3,000 to 3,500. In addition to the ongoing use of boardinghouses designed for single men, employees had the option of leasing land from the company and constructing their own houses or constructing homes on private property away from the facility, although this meant a longer walk to and from work. Another common housing option was for the primary occupant to take in boarders; this relieved the companies of the need for more housing and provided auxiliary income for the primary occupants. Even so, there were fewer company houses than employees who desired them. Eligibility for a company house depended on one's status with the employer. The higher the position in the workplace hierarchy or the more valuable an employee you were perceived, the more likely you were to obtain a house, and the better house you would receive. More elaborate homes were specifically designed and granted to managerial and supervisory staff with niceties such as closets, more rooms and embellishments such as woodworked finishing on the exterior or interior.

Communities were frequently (but not always) organized into sections: industrial buildings, laborers' homes and managers' homes. Compounding the complexity of the social milieu were the ethnic overtones for employee assignments. Later immigrants with limited English, such as Finns, Italians and Croatians (lumped with Slovenes as Austrians from the Austro-Hungarian empire), were assigned less-skilled positions in the workplace and, consequentially, were on the bottom rung of the housing pecking order.

Calumet and Hecla houses were rented to employees. *Michigan Tech Archives.*

The company's return on investment with the houses appears to have been low. Rather than being viewed as a significant revenue stream, they were perceived as a method of rewarding and influencing employees. Certainly employee requests for home repairs and occupancy and from those who wanted to "move up" to a house with more amenities were major distractions for the unlucky official who had to handle the inquiries.

Maintenance for the houses, such as roof repair, was normally performed by the companies; however, it appears to have been a frequent issue of contention between tenant/employee and landlord/employer. Home repair and construction were normally accomplished by the carpentry department of the company, although some house construction was outsourced from time to time. Companies would typically provide heating fuel at minimal cost, depending on the primary type used by the company, coal or wood. At the Atlantic Mine, electrical power came to the residential area thirty years after it was used in the mines. Charges were levied by some companies for both the wire used to deliver the power and the poles needed support the wire. Many families had small vegetable gardens and kept dairy cows. In some cases, the company rented vegetable gardens and pasturage for the cattle.

Arne Anderson described his family's experience at the Menard Mine. His father walked four miles to the mine and used skis when the weather was terrible in the winter. In addition to his blacksmith work at the mine, he worked his farm with a cow, a horse and chickens. He grew potatoes, turnips and carrots. When his brothers could no longer find work in the mines, they obtained employment at Michigan Technological University in Houghton, performing electrical and maintenance work.

The actual work performed by mine employees was, to say the least, arduous, dirty and dangerous. It began with a long descent into the mine, working in cramped, dark conditions that were very physically demanding and dangerous. Initially, mine access involved the use of a series of ladders; later, the ascent and decent were mechanized with a "mechanical ladder" or elevator-type apparatus. Miners worked with drilling tools that could easily cause accidents (nearly all mines had a physician on hand to treat wounds), and explosives could ignite prematurely or in a delayed fashion, causing injury. All of this was done under very poor illumination, initially by candlelight. Deeper mines were also damp and warm, and ventilation was a chronic problem. "Trammers," those who loaded tram carts with stone and then moved them to the mine shaft, were often compared to beasts of burden. A few mines used mules to assist in the transport. Above ground, the rock had to be handled again, crushed and passed through multi-stage sorting processes that used water in separating ore from waste rock. This dust and dirt tended to stay with the laborers and their clothing, as bathing facilities were primitive. It was not uncommon, especially in earlier locations, for miners to have to furnish their own tools, explosive paraphernalia and candles.

Employees were identified and paid based on their tasks, as well as whether they worked above ground or underground. Below-ground miners did the actual drilling, trammers the hauling and timber men the installation of support timbers and braces. (The mining companies used much of the "first cut" of Upper Peninsula forests below ground.) The support the timbers provided was a necessity although also viewed as a fire risk. The rock-laden nature of the underground cavities meant that less support was needed than in some other mining locations. Some mines employed boys as young as twelve to sort rock and run errands underground. Their pay ran from one-half to two-thirds of the normal minimum wage. Miners were frequently paid as "contract" workers whose compensation was calculated by the distance (feet or fathoms) they progressed. Mine payment was to the miner teams rather than directly to individuals. Another system, also inherited from Cornwall,

The Atlantic Mining Company Store was located in Redridge, west of Hancock and Houghton. *Michigan Tech Archives.*

was the "tribute" system, normally implemented when a mine was closing out. Individual miners were paid on the value of the ore they delivered to the surface. When the ore vein ran in a vertical and angular direction (which was frequently the case), called a stope, the drilling was especially challenging. Other employee wages were calculated by the day: initially a ten-hour day, it was gradually reduced to nine and eventually eight hours.

Companies supported communities' recreational, medical, educational and religious institutions. Calumet and Hecla and Copper Range constructed large libraries that also functioned somewhat as community centers. They provided not only books and newspapers in both English and non-English languages but also meeting and recreation rooms and bathhouses in the basements. Library reading selections ranged from popular to scholarly in languages from Norwegian to Croatian.

The development of the company hospital was an outgrowth of the mine physician and an expanded sophistication of medical practice. Employees were usually charged one dollar per month for medical care that included their families. Whereas each mine would typically have one doctor, the hospital would tend to serve several mining communities.

The development of public schools was generally supported by the mining companies. Typically, at the very least, they donated land on which the building could be constructed. They certainly monitored school activities, as they were the largest taxpayers in the district and wanted to be represented on the school boards. Their self-interest was focused on increasing English language skills and keeping the need for tax assessments low. Inside the schools, teachers were challenged with students raised in many languages. Initial schools had a short school year of three to six months and a maximum grade of six or eight. When high schools appeared later, they frequently served several communities, such as the one at Atlantic Mine. It was not unusual for such students to take a train to school.

Although many mining companies had general merchandise stores (especially in the earliest years), the practice was not universal. Calumet and Hecla avoided the practice, evidently because it wanted to keep its focus on mine production, and it wanted to avoid the ill will that frequently came with company management of the stores. Copper Range had many stores but withdrew from the practice as alternatives presented themselves. Common practice was for a weekly order to be taken and then delivered to homes, although a storefront service was also provided. Stores were open to residents who were not employees. Where company store ownership didn't exist, influence certainly did. Typically, the companies leased the land to the store and "leaned" on it to keep prices low and prohibit the sale of liquor. Perhaps the more "hands off" approach explains the popular and successful development of the Tamarack Co-operative Association Store near Calumet.

Popular recreational activities enjoyed by the locals included baseball teams from the various communities and some of the country's first professional ice hockey teams from Calumet and Houghton. Like many new communities in the United States, residents demonstrated great excitement in celebrating the Fourth of July. Fraternal organizations, which were frequently defined along ethnic lines, were front and center in the parades, but they also sponsored a variety of social gatherings from dances to concerts and plays throughout the year. Some benefit societies also sponsored insurance programs that provided a limited "safety net" for employees during times of illness, death or disability. In many cases, the company was a participant in such programs, either as a board member or in providing some funding. Disability payments normally had a time limit, and death benefits were done in lump-sum dispersion.

Churches were encouraged by the mining companies, as they were seen as an antidote to the too-frequent male pastimes of drinking and fighting. These behaviors negatively affected their productivity on the job. The first clergy who arrived in the area were sent as missionaries to the Native

Americans. They were encouraged to expand their services to the miners. The first denominations tended to be Roman Catholic (favored by the French Canadian and German employees) and Methodist, with which the Cornish were familiar. Other common groups in the Copper Country were Lutherans and temperance societies. One company was so eager to subdue the raucous behavior of its employees that it actually paid the salary of the clergy. The most common practice, however, was to lease or donate land for the construction of a church.

Company influence affected the community away from the workplace. At Atlantic Mine (both a town and a mine, which was purchased by Copper Range), located eight miles west of Houghton, elections were heavily influenced by mining officials. As recounted by John Kolehmainen, voters had to ask for a Democratic or Republican ballot. Election workers employed by the mine made their preference and expectations for Republican candidates clear. For years, election results in the Keweenaw were heavily Republican. Sandra Hollingsworth stated that asking for the Democratic ballot put your job at the mine in jeopardy.

The Copper Range Company was unique in its development of a major railroad line of significant length (many companies had short lines

Calumet and Hecla's bathhouse. *Michigan Tech Archives.*

to support their movement of rock to and from their mills and smelters) and its other ventures. They gained control of the C.G. Hussy Company in Pittsburgh, whose business was fabricating copper products—most mining companies' association with the mineral ended with the shipping of copper bar or ingots. The Copper Range also developed a bus service and electric power company that eventually developed into the major electric provider in the Upper Peninsula. Company operation of an icehouse and ice service was also common throughout the area.

The formation of unions in the copper district was either late in coming or nonexistent. Although there would be job walkouts from time to time, frequently initiated by a department or employee groups, it was not until 1913 that an organized effort by the Western Federation of Miners led to an area-wide nine-month strike. Prior efforts by the Knights of Labor to organize the mine employees had been unsuccessful. WFM union issues were union recognition, wages, an eight-hour day, grievance procedures and implementation of the one-man drill. (A change from the two-man drill meant fewer jobs for miners, and a lone miner was perceived as a safety issue.) Many writers of the day pronounced that the area was a model of labor peace and satisfaction. The length and intensity of the strike that followed would indicate that such notions were a little short of the full truth. The companies had employed private security forces to discourage union activity and utilized spies in the workforce, and in the end, the Michigan National Guard held a major presence during the strike. Lives were lost and scab labor was brought in; it all culminated in the terrible deaths of seventy-three (most of them children) at the Christmas Eve party at the Italian Hall.

Intransience in labor negotiations was fueled by the companies' struggle with low copper prices, increased competition from copper mines in the West and determination not to accept unionization. Workers' concerns were a lack of equity with western miners' wages and the threat of job loss due to the introduction of the one-man drill. In the end, the company won on all issues, although the workday was eventually shortened. Was the company town structure an issue? Apparently not, except that perhaps in the companies' minds they were already giving the employees the advantages of low-cost housing and other benefits that were unappreciated or unrecognized.

In some respect, the strike marked the beginning of a long, gradual decline in the copper industry of the area, although it could also be said that the decline had already begun and fueled the turmoil of the strike. One by one, the mines either cut back, closed or consolidated, with subsequent reductions in employment. Low copper prices and greater competition from open-pit mines in the West and overseas contributed, as did the Depression and dwindling supplies of copper in the Keweenaw mines. The one exception was the boom period during World War I. With lower opportunity for employment in the Keweenaw and greater opportunity and better wages in other growing regions, such as Detroit's automobile industry, the population began a long decline. Over time, the demand and need for company housing was reduced, and companies began selling off houses, frequently to occupants who had been renting and at low cost, usually under $1,000. A common practice was to sell the house but retain rights to the property through a long-term lease. Mining operations for the big three companies in the area terminated in or fell to minimal production or reclamation levels in the 1950s, '60s and '70s.

Today, the communities of Calumet, Hancock and Houghton have more diversified economic bases built on higher education, manufacturing shops, small businesses, medical services, forestry, recreation and tourism. A renewed interest in copper mining was sparked in 2014 by exploratory drilling by the Canadian Highland Copper Company twenty miles northeast of Calumet, not far from the original copper mines in the Keweenaw Peninsula. The area's mining history is well preserved and interpreted through the Keweenaw National Historic Park in Hancock and Calumet, along with many public and private mines and museums.

FORD RIVER

The small community of Ford River took its name from the former Illinois governor and investor Thomas Ford, who first took an interest in developing a lumber mill where the river flowed into Lake Michigan. Located just nine miles southwest of Escanaba in the midst of a white pine and cedar forest, several lumber mills passed from the scene over a period of twenty years before the Ford River Lumber Company established itself in 1862. The new co-owners resided in Illinois and Wisconsin. Captain John McDonald was the early on-site manager. After its first mill was destroyed by fire, three additional steam-operated mills were constructed nearer to the mouth of the river, away from the original town site, what was called Uppertown. Additional harvest from the area included hemlock, spruce and basswood.

The company had complete ownership of the mills, boardinghouse/hotel, store/office building, sleeping house, restaurant, general warehouse, homes, barns, town hall, community privy, logging camps and three schooners to transport the finished products to the Chicago area. A tugboat was used to help maneuver the many schooners and barges to the seven company docks. Many other vessels (some reports of as many as thirty at a time) took loads of lumber, railroad ties, laths, posts and shingles to other Great Lakes ports. In some cases, shipments arrived from other logging facilities or were taken to Escanaba. Reports have estimates of between seven hundred and one thousand people employed with the lumber company, along with some independent farmers in the area and a Native American community south of town. These latter two groups were employed in the loading of the vessels. They were paid fifty cents per day until the longshoremen's union in Chicago got wind of it and insisted they join the union. Thereafter they were paid fifty cents per hour.

Mill laborers worked in the logging camps during the winter and with the log drive in the spring. During the winter, when the men were logging, the women could make purchases at the company's store "on account." Unused balances could be "settled up" when the loggers returned in the late spring. Reports are that there was rarely a balance for settling. At other times during the year, wages were paid in coupons that could be redeemed at the company store. The store originally carried only groceries and meat shipped in from Chicago. Later, a full inventory of household items was added that included furniture, men's work apparel, yard goods and other household items. As the number of area farms developed, so did local food sources, reducing the need for the company farm. Water service from a nearby spring could be purchased from the company, as could firewood. Many families supplemented their incomes by renting out space in their homes.

Other facilities in the village included a nondenominational church, a public school and Skandia Hall, where dances and other social and entertainment events were held, including plays, bazaars and performances of the community band. There was no local physician; such services were available in Escanaba.

As the supplies of timber ran out, the facilities were sold to the I. Stephenson Company, which operated a mill in Wells on the north side of Escanaba. In 1912, the facilities and major land assets were liquidated. In 2015, the area has one restaurant/bar, one retail business, a campground and a collection of residential and resort properties.

FAYETTE

Considered by many as one of the Upper Peninsula's most picturesque locales, Fayette became a noisy, smoke-filled industrial town center and one of the area's first company towns in 1867. The Jackson Iron Company began its mining operations in the Negaunee area in the 1850s and was serious about identifying a less costly method of transporting its iron ore to the steel-making centers in Ohio and Illinois. Shipping bulk iron ore, complete with its impurities, was costly despite the opening of the locks at Sault Ste. Marie. Jackson manager Fayette Brown was charged with identifying a new port on Lake Michigan near the terminus of the new Peninsula Railroad line that ran from Negaunee to Escanaba. The Snail Shell Harbor, two-thirds of the way out on the twenty-mile Garden Peninsula, had just what he was looking for: available hardwood forests and waterway access. The adjacent dolomite limestone cliffs were an added bonus, as was the sheltered and deep-water nature of the harbor cove, which was named Fayette after the founder. The Jackson Iron Company was one of the first major mining companies in the Upper Peninsula; begun in downstate Jackson, its headquarters was later moved to Cleveland.

Construction of industrial and domestic facilities began in May 1867 and was quickly shaping up by the end of the year. Iron ore was shipped by rail from the Negaunee area to Escanaba, where it was transferred by ship the twenty-five miles to Fayette. There it was crushed and combined with similarly crushed limestone and charcoal in furnaces, where it was superheated into a molten form. After it was separated from the waste slag, it was poured into one-

This reproduced log house at Fayette was the type of housing common for most laborers. *Photo by author.*

hundred-pound molds or "pigs" for hardening. The pig iron was then shipped to the steel mills in Ohio or Chicago. Two major blast furnaces were the focus of the production; attached to them were steam furnaces that superheated air that was blown into the "blast" furnaces to melt the mixture, which had been dropped into the top of the furnaces. Support facilities included storehouses, charcoal kilns, a lime kiln, a machine shop, a blacksmith shop, a roundhouse and a sawmill with connecting carpentry shops and company offices. Because of the community's isolation, many necessary items had to be manufactured or repaired on-site in the machine, carpentry or blacksmith's shops: parts for the machinery, wagons for moving the charcoal or iron, barges and wheelbarrows for moving the ore, tools and so on. The steam-powered crusher and sawmill added to the noise generated by the blasting done to extract the limestone. Immediately adjacent to the town were the white limestone cliffs, which were mined; a "scale pit" was used to weigh items such as charcoal and other items purchased or sold, and along the beach was a "slag beach" where waste (cinder-like) byproducts from the furnace were dumped.

Domestic facilities at Fayette included cabins for laborers, frame homes for management personnel, a boardinghouse, a hotel, a general store, a meat market, residences for the superintendent and doctor and a town hall. Other features of the town included an icehouse, a granary, a livestock barn, a jail, a schoolhouse, a half-mile horse racing track with a baseball field and the Catholic St. Peter's Church and its cemetery. Cabins for ordinary laborers were very small (three hundred square feet) and primitive, hardly more than one-room, one-story structures with no floors. Many families took in boarders to generate more income. Single men lived in the boardinghouse. Department heads lived in frame houses with windows and stone foundations. A central water line was run for firefighting and to service the hotel and livery. Otherwise, water had to be hauled from the bay, and reports indicate that it was cloudy due to the limestone mining nearby. The hotel had a second-story privy to accommodate those not on the first floor.

Another unique industrial dimension was the role of charcoal production in the Fayette complex. The high heat–producing quality of the charcoal was developed from the hardwoods of the area: beach, maple and ironwood. Logs were cut into four-foot lengths and then burned slowly for six to eight days in

Reconstructed Fayette kilns as were used for producing charcoal. *Photo by author.*

mounds or, later, kilns. The mounds were called pits and were thirty to forty feet in diameter and eight to ten feet in height and could contain twenty-five to thirty cords of wood. The stone kilns that resembled an inverted cone or an igloo had the same diameter but were twice as high. Bushels ("scuttle baskets," made by local Native American women) of charcoal were then transported by wagon to the Fayette complex; later, a six-mile narrow-gauge railroad was constructed for such. Kiln sites near the lake shipped by small vessel. The mounds were constructed by piling the wood and then covering it with dirt and green leaves. The "slow burn" was accomplished by controlling the airflow. There were more than fifty of these charcoal-burning locations scattered around the Garden Peninsula—each resembled a tiny village, with cabins, a livery, a large scale, a carpentry shop and, in some cases, a bar or small store. Some operated as contracted "satellites" of the Fayette facility, and some were privately owned. Those that were contracted were expected to operate under company guidelines.

Fayette had more than nine hundred feet of dockage. At least three steamers were occupied with transporting the pig iron to the southern Great Lakes regions. Two tugs were occupied with six barges running to and from Escanaba carrying iron ore and other supplies needed for the town or factory. The Fayette railroad included two engines, ten charcoal cars, ten logging cars and two flatcars. The rail line was later expanded to the end of the peninsula.

The Fayette facility truly flourished both industrially (it became one of the most productive producers of pig iron in the Upper Peninsula) and socially (the number of employees rose to four hundred and perhaps five hundred in the surrounding area). The hotel was named the Sheldon House and developed to attract tourists with its décor and amenities that compared favorably with those found in major cities of the era. The Fayette Dramatic Society performed in the "Opera House," as did touring entertainers and minstrel shows. The Opera House hosted debates, lectures and concerts. Dances were held, both formal and shindigs. The uniformed Fayette Cornet Band performed locally and in neighboring communities for special events. The baseball team traveled to Manistique and Escanaba. Steamships connected to Escanaba four times per week, and coaches ran over the ice in the winter. The longer overland trip by stagecoach from Escanaba to Fayette was a two-day trip. An Odd Fellows Lodge was formed along with a Fayette Agricultural Society. Other denominations held services on a regular basis in either the hotel or town hall, Methodist and Congregational alike.

These restored houses at Fayette were occupied by supervisory staff. *Photo by author.*

The company store contained a wide inventory that was complemented by a fresh meat market. The store's items included groceries, hardware, clothing, yard goods, housewares and tobacco products. The market and many other businesses in town were not operated by the company but rather rented from the company and had to abide by its guidelines. Business owners and employees had to sign a contract indicating their willingness to abide by the rules and regulations stipulated. Consensus seems to have been that purchasing from mail-order catalogues was a less expensive option than the local store. Basic laborers were paid one dollar per day, and those in skilled positions such as teamsters, machinists or the blacksmith made more than twice that amount. Employees were paid once a month, and their wages were balanced against charges from the store, meat market, medical service and rent. Indications are that such balances were quite low. Additional businesses also appeared on the scene, including a barbershop, a livery, a photo gallery, a small art gallery and a life insurance agent.

The area around Fayette began to develop as well. The number of farms increased, and the commercial fishing industry grew, with shipments of whitefish and trout to Chicago. On-site, company lime was exported on schooners or steamships, as were telegraph poles. Heartfelt and colorful stories became part of the Fayette legacy. One German immigrant had saved funds for bringing the wife he'd left behind in the old country. When he got to Chicago on his way to retrieve her, he was robbed and returned home penniless and without the frau. The townsfolk raised the funds, and the couple was happily reunited. When the town of Peshtigo burned at about the time of the Chicago fire, the Fayette folks raised a large donation to assist it. Although vice was controlled in Fayette through the company's authority, the area around the town was not without "dives," where all forms of alcohol or female companionship could be purchased.

Establishments such as Hole in the Wall provide a sense of the degree of unsavory characters who operated such. On one occasion, a young woman showed up in town asking where an individual lived. She was responding to an employment advertisement in the Chicago paper for someone to assist his wife, who was in poor health. Townsfolk directed her but were suspicious, as they knew the man had no wife; he did, however, have several women on-site whose services were available for purchase. A week later, she was discovered

Surviving blast furnace structures at Fayette are impressive. *Photo by author.*

along the roadway, having been badly beaten. A group descended on the site and ransacked it, dividing the large sum of money located there among the beaten woman and four others discovered there and sending them all on their way. The owner was beaten either to death or just to the edge of it (accounts vary) but was never seen in the area again. There are also accounts that female companionship and alcoholic refreshments could be found on small ships that frequented the area, safely offshore from the Jackson Iron Company's authority. One such character was the infamous pirate captain Dan Seavey.

The 1891 decline of the Jackson Iron facility in Fayette was the result of several factors. It was discovered that a comparable quality of steel could be produced nearer the steel mills with coke or coal-fueled furnaces, the supply of immediately available hardwood was dwindling and the aging of the industrial facilities was going to require significant financial investment for restoring and upgrading. The Cleveland Cliffs Iron Company eventually gained ownership when it bought out the Jackson Iron Company's holdings. A series of private owners attempted to revive the harbor area as a resort, with limited success. Finally, the State of Michigan obtained ownership, and the Conservation Department (later the DNR) partnered with the state's history division to develop it as a recreation center and a restored town site. It now operates as Fayette Historic State Park, with a variety of recreational venues such as camping and hiking. Ongoing archaeological and restoration activities enhance the presentation of the town to re-create how it appeared in the late 1800s. The Garden area's economy today is based on agriculture, tourism, recreation, forestry and commercial fishing.

PEQUAMING

Pequaming is unique in a variety of ways. At one time, it was the largest lumber-producing mill in the Upper Peninsula, yet now it has virtually no industry. Over time, the town was owned by two different companies with dramatically different styles. And it also has a very odd geography, resting on a knob-shaped peninsula sticking out into Keweenaw Bay of Lake Superior. The first visitors and occupants of the area were Native Americans, with indications of their living in the area as far back as the year 1000. Ojibwa tribes from Canada were followed by the Sioux, Menominis, Ottawas and Hurons as many moved on westward. With Europeans came a fur trading post to the location, as well as missionaries, both Methodist and Catholic. The story of Pequaming is well told through the publications of Brian Cleven and a joint account by Earle Doyle and Ruth MacFarlane.

Charles W. Hebard, who had some background in the New York lumber industry, saw the potential in 1878 and purchased 100,000 acres in the Upper Peninsula. He proceeded to construct a steam-powered lumber mill and shingle mills at Pequaming, so named from the Native American term, *Pequaquawaming* ("point village" or "cape point"). Those were accompanied with the eventual construction of one hundred homes, two boardinghouses, a general store, a post office and a water supply with hydrants system. Extensive docks were also constructed not only for the ships and barges but also to store logs or lumber that were in transit. The town grew rapidly, with 240 employed at the mills, 400 in seventeen logging camps and completion of a school and church. Most logs were pulled by tugs to the mill along the lake. Along with lumber production were shingles, rail ties, lathes and hemlock bark used by tanneries. From Pequaming, lumber was rafted eight miles to L'Anse. From there, it left by vessel or via the Marquette, Houghton and Ontonagon Railroad to the south. After a railroad was installed later as a feeder for hardwoods from the camps to Pequaming, loaded rail cars of logs were floated to Baraga, seven miles across the bay, for milling.

All buildings in town were company owned, but all occupants, who paid one dollar per year for rent, were responsible for their upkeep. A hotel was added, as was a town hall that functioned as a recreation center for dances and entertainment, with an Odd Fellows Lodge on the second floor. The company provided whitewash for the picket fences around town, and pedestrians had use of planked sidewalks. Many early employees were Canadians or American-born. Later, there were European immigrants, some Native Americans and some African Americans. Enough Finns moved down from the Keweenaw Peninsula for there to be designated a portion of town called Finntown; there was also a Finnish athletic club. The company facilitated setting aside funds to finance passage for wives and family members from Europe. Annual social events included the Pequaming Fair and the Native American summer church camp meetings. These derived from the tradition established by the early Methodist missionaries in the area. In a weeklong session, preachers came from other areas of Michigan, Wisconsin and Minnesota, and participants slept in rustic cabins or tents. Participants were not limited to Native Americans. Three churches were constructed—St. Joseph's Catholic Church, Finnish Lutheran and a Union church—to accommodate a variety of denominational backgrounds.

The Pequaming community's economic and social texture continued to develop. Fishing was a strong local industry, and area farms also developed. Evidently, the bugs and vegetation that fell off the logs in the harbor were a delicacy for area fish, which thrived and yielded a plentiful harvest. The town did not have a local doctor until 1906; otherwise, the services were on-call from L'Anse. The town continued to grow, peaking at eight hundred in 1897. The town was considered attractive not only for its natural setting on the lake but also for its design, with wide streets and wood-frame houses. Many existing trees had been left when the town site was laid out. Electrical power was in place by the 1880s, as was telephone service, although service was certainly not universal. Priorities were for the Hebard residence and the company office. A Pequaming Club was organized to promote the community and its social life through education and cultural activities for the public and youth (fundraisers, plays and trips). There was a community

Sawmill at Pequaming. *Michigan Tech Archives.*

orchestra and a band, along with athletic activities for adults and children, such as hockey and baseball. The clubhouse had a bowling alley, billiards and a library. One recreational option not available was a tavern, although there were reports of travel to neighboring communities, homebrewing and blind pigs. The company sponsored a Christmas party at the town hall and distributed presents for the children.

Lumber cut at Pequaming was considered of high quality due to its method of feeding logs through the saws. Logs were rotated before sawing to sync the wood grain with the cut. Years later, with new owners, the priority became maximum plank yield rather than the quality of the board. The standard-gauge railroad was twenty-three miles long and ran to logging camps east of Pequaming. It included three locomotives, three log loaders, eighty-five "Russell" log cars and one snow plow. This was installed when the switch was made to include cutting hardwoods that could not be easily floated in the lake.

Pequaming after the Ford purchase included a new water tower and extensive grounds cleanup. *Michigan Tech Archives.*

After Charles W. Hebard died, his sons eventually decided that the logging industry's days were numbered, and they sold the facility to Henry Ford, who was looking to expand his timber holdings in the Upper Peninsula. In September 1923, the sale was completed, and Ford began an intensive makeover and retrofit of the Pequaming mill and town. Equipment was upgraded, homes were remodeled and everything got a good scrubbing and paint job. Employees had to pass a physical exam to qualify as Ford employees. Those long-term Hebard employees who were not hired by Ford were given pensions by the Heberds. The casual work style of the past was shaken up with the use of time cards and the termination of the use of children sorting or piling in the wood yard. Rates of pay nearly doubled, but livestock (cows, chickens and pigs) was removed from town due to sanitary concerns. Ford encouraged vegetable gardens, though. Home rental jumped to twelve to fifteen dollars per month, but employees were making more and quality of housing was perceived as having increased dramatically. The water supply system was upgraded and expanded for enhanced firefighting capability, and a fire truck was added. Shingle and lath production was terminated, but a planing mill was added. The waste wood burner that looked like a silo was torn down, and a 120,000-gallon water tower was erected complete with the Ford logo. The Pequaming railroad was connected with the Ford rail line to facilitate log and lumber transfer with the L'Anse Ford facility. Prices in the company store were considered low, so much so that non-employees had to be scurried away. Fences were torn down to provide a neater-looking village, and houses were re-shingled. Along with the increased importance placed on the appearance of the community came Ford's more emphatic prohibition on drinking and his promotion of building personal savings accounts. The store provided groceries, clothing and yard goods; milk, cheese and meats were to be acquired from local farmers. Building supplies, appliances and furniture had to be acquired from L'Anse.

Henry Ford's interest in schools played out well for the children in Pequaming. He constructed four one-room elementary buildings and a high school. Although officially part of the L'Anse Township Schools, they functioned as private schools, with Ford picking up the costs for supplies and salaries. His progressive stamp came through on the curriculum, as it included homemaking classes and trade shops, both woodworking and metal. Children from outside Pequaming could attend if a parent was a Ford employee. The shops had the latest power tools, along with a photography lab, drafting tables and a school newspaper. Ford also promoted all forms of dancing and enjoyed participating with the children when he visited town. Unfortunately, Ford's involvement in the high school lasted only four years, until the corporate activities began winding down at Pequaming.

Finished lumber left on Ford boats for lower Michigan, New Jersey or Pennsylvania. Most was used to crate automobile products. With the Depression, car sales plummeted and, with them, the demand for Pequaming's product. Employees were kept busy developing an eight-hundred-acre farm for residents. The Ford Motor Company donated shoes and clothing to employees during the Depression; however, the decline of Pequaming was well on its way. The store closed in 1937. World War II contributed with its manpower needs and rationing of rubber for tires

Movement of logs and lumber between Ford sites at Pequaming, Baraga and L'Anse utilized lake transport on barges, as seen in this 1927 photo. *Michigan Tech Archives.*

After the Ford departure from Pequaming, it went on the list of ghost towns. Photo from 1964. *Michigan Tech Archives.*

needed for the trucks that were now critical for Pequaming's industry. The infrastructure of Pequaming was deteriorating, in the minds of Ford officials, especially housing and related sanitation issues. Indications are that the closing of Pequaming's operations in 1942, and the effect on the community, broke Henry Ford's heart. However, he was eighty-nine at the time and not steering the corporate ship.

When Ford Motor Company sold off Pequaming in 1952, it was purchased by a group of investors who hoped to develop it as a recreation and resort area. Several attempts to accomplish such have fallen short. Today, it does have some seasonal and resort homes (both new construction and restored), some historic buildings and some deteriorating structures. Adjacent to Pequaming is the largest and oldest reservation in the state of Michigan: the L'Anse Indian Reservation, home of the Lake Superior Band of Chippewa Indians.

HERMANSVILLE

When Charles Julius Ludwig Meyer determined that the logging supply in the forests of Wisconsin near Fond du Luc was not adequate for his Wisconsin Land and Lumber Company in 1877, he began surveying northern Michigan. Normally called "CJ" or "alphabet Meyer" due to his insistence on the use of all his named initials, he was born in Prussia and was introduced to wood industries by his father, a cabinetmaker. A strongly motivated and talented individual (as a mathematician and inventor of mechanical devices), he left Europe at age eighteen and found employment in New York State and Chicago before settling in Fond du Lac in eastern Wisconsin, called "the Winnebego Valley" area. There he developed a small but substantial industrial and financial empire, with two hundred employees who produced lumber, shingles, doors, blinds, sashes, axe handles, washboards and cabinetry. CJ was quite an entrepreneur, a man who tried a blast furnace operation that never thrived and a civic leader who became mayor of Fond du Lac.

In Michigan, he found an area with the convergence of three features he sought: plentiful forests, the Little Cedar River and the Chicago and North Western Railway. The district was situated in northern Menominee County, where some pine logging had been done after the area had been vacated by the Menominee Native Americans. He purchased his first land there in 1878, and his sawmill was operating by 1879. Along with the sawmill, the first buildings included a large warehouse, a boardinghouse (constructed from a dismantled shingle mill from Fond du Lac) and small houses for married employees. The houses contained a small bedroom, a dining/kitchen area and an open dorm/attic area above. The location needed a name, and CJ's son, Herman, became the namesake for Hermansville. Later, a separate township was formed and named for the benefactor, Meyer; he continued to manage his Michigan operation from Fond du Lac, 180 miles to the south.

Early developments in Hermansville included a strike (and the first blacklist) and worker turnover as they weighed rates of pay and working conditions between the forests and newly opened area mines on the Menominee Iron Range, employee illnesses and sanitation issues and construction of more boardinghouses and family homes. Compensation was eighteen to twenty dollars per month, with a sixty-cent deduction for room and board if someone didn't work on that day. At one point, the interiors of the boardinghouses had to be plastered to control the lice. It was common for wood workers, whose major work was done in the winter, to work on the company farms during the summer months. These farms produced valuable fodder for the many horses and livestock, as well as produce for the logging camps. Another early major community issue that developed was the establishment of a house of prostitution near Hermansville. Company officials wanted to put a stop to it, along with the sale of alcohol that went with it. The company hired Pinkerton detectives to document activities there and then turned the evidence over to the Menominee County district attorney's office for charging and prosecuting. An offshoot of this was the decision of Wisconsin Land and Lumber to allow a tavern in Hermansville where the drinking could be more controlled.

The Hermansville operation continued to expand beyond production of lumber, posts and shingles. Lime was processed and charcoal produced in beehive-shaped kilns for area iron production to the west. As many as twelve railroad cars loaded with lumber left each day for Chicago and Fond du Lac, Meyer's other facilities. Meanwhile, he had encouraged officials of the Minneapolis, Sault Ste. Marie and Atlantic Railway (later to become the Soo Line) to run through Hermansville. This was quite unusual for a small town to have two railroad lines servicing it. Later, some lumber sales were made "in the Dakota territory." Meyer initiated the Hermansville and Western Railroad to bring in logs from camps to the mills in Hermansville. Such operations were notorious for winding around hills and valleys to diminish construction costs, but this evidently rose to a new level and was called the "Hell, Western and Crooked." Not all Meyer's ventures turned to gold, however. An oft-repeated story was his plan to save money by raising his own pigs in the basement of a building. Evidently, the cool and damp conditions were not favorable for the pigs, and they all died. During the life of the Hermansville mills, there were as many as forty logging camps that developed and then dissolved as the useable tress were cut off. The immediate area for developing the town site was quite rough, and considerable earth had to be moved to make it suitable.

C.J.L. Meyer's daughter married Dr. George Earle. Meyer had convinced Earle to move to Hermansville for a rest from his busy medical practice in New York State. Soon thereafter, the Panic of 1889, a major economic depression, forced Meyer into bankruptcy, and he lost his Fond du Lac and Chicago operations. Earle took over the Hermansville operation, and it thrived under his direction for many years. Meyer had been respected for his expertise as an inventor and in financial developments; however, he was ensconced in Wisconsin and not as connected with the Hermansville operations and community as Earle became.

Significant reductions in the pine forests had occurred by area loggers before the establishment of the Hermansville mills. The future of Hermansville depended on use of the hardwoods. This had led to pursuit of charcoal production in the earliest years. Hemlock bark was sought by the tanneries in their processing of leather (there were major tanneries in Manistique and the Sault). However, the real salvation for Hermansville was in the production of high-quality hardwood floors. Before Meyer's innovations, hardwoods floors had to be finished when installed on-site. The machinery he developed and patented produced tongue-and-groove maple flooring that was completely finished and needed no further sanding when laid. The excellent product led to the "IXL" branding that became the Hermansville hallmark. Sales were made nationally and around the world, the most famous installation being in the Mormon Temple in Salt Lake City. One story that indicates its national reputation is delivery of a letter from New Zealand, addressed simply "IXL Company, USA." There were reports of industrial espionage from competitors who wanted to replicate IXL production techniques and machinery. One such presented himself as a job applicant but was actually working for a Grand Rapids firm. One local rival for both product sales and laborers was the I. Stephenson Company in Wells, with which the pay scales were often compared.

As the number of employees grew to four hundred by 1884, the number of buildings grew significantly from the first mill, boardinghouse, warehouse and homes. Added were several mills (cedar/pine, tie, planing, hardwood and flooring, firewood and feed and flour), boiler house, engine shop, two churches (Methodist Episcopal and Catholic), barns, drying kilns, meat market, jail/post office, icehouse, theater/opera house, clubhouse, more warehouses and, later, an electric light plant and bank. Elevated tramways were used for moving finished lumber around the "yard" area for sorting, storage or drying. There were four different stores, as some succumbed to fire. Normally, throughout most of the community's history, there was both a company store and one not affiliated with the company. After the company constructed the first school (when the adjacent Spaulding School Board initially refused to establish one for Hermansville children), two additional school buildings followed. Eventually, a separate school district was formed: Meyer Township Schools, more commonly called Hermansville schools. Both the Chicago and North Western and Soo Line Railroads had their own depots. There were two hotels, the Hotel Menominee in 1911 and the Hotel Herman in 1890. The latter was indeed short-lived, as it burned down the night before its grand opening; it must have been heart-wrenching for the owners, as it was to be promoted as the grandest facility in the Upper Peninsula. Evidently, workmen putting finishing touches on the facility accidently caused the fire. The Hermansville "complex" also included farms, a quarry and a "hot pond" for preparing the logs for the sawmill.

The backgrounds of residents were quite varied: initially Germans, Scandinavians and Canadians and, later, more Austrians (primarily Croatians) and Italians. There were also some of Czech and Slovene descent. One community survey indicated that half of the residents were born outside the United States and half inside. Some had the price of passage from Europe paid by the company, with the understanding that they would "work it off" once employed. Many resided in like-minded neighborhoods, such as "Little Italy," Frenchtown, Germantown or the Swedish settlement. There was a poor farm (called the County Farm) and a Pest House for those with contagious diseases. Three former Pest Houses were designated for the Croatians. Frank Kobasic described his as a four-apartment building that had one window and one light bulb per apartment. Census records indicate his residence as Croatian Settlement No. 2. Less formal was a "hobo jungle" area for tramps who had arrived in town on the trains but who hadn't found employment. With multiple rail lines running through Hermansville, this was a frequent occurrence. It was not uncommon for some to appear at back doors looking for free meals.

Outside the workplace, the social life of the community focused around the post office ("What's the news?"), train depots ("Who's coming or going?") or the stores ("Who's buying what?"). Lodges (the Austrian Hall) and fraternal organizations reinforced nationalistic bonds, such as Sons of Venezia (Italian). Despite strong ties to their homeland, the Fourth of July celebration was a time for showing off one's patriotism. Parade entries included Boy Scouts, Girl Scouts, 4-H, Knights of Pythias (a fraternal organization not too different from the Masons), Woodmen of America (fraternal organization of those employed in the wood products industry) and the National Croatian Society. Local music was provided by the Italian and Croatian bands who staged competitions and played at dances and celebrations. One of the more unique organizations was the Royal Neighbor Society, which provided insurance and annuity programs for women.

The company town structure of Wisconsin Land and Lumber in Hermansville led to unusual arrangements in the community. For example, because the company was the only taxpayer, it was able to exert both real and implied influence over all types of affairs. Company officials were in primary positions on county, township and school district boards. The township hired a night watchman whose responsibilities were overseeing the goings-on around the mill at night. Reports varied from drinking and gambling on the job to suspicious characters arriving on the train. The barber paid thirty dollars per month rent to the company for locating his shop on IXL property. The company hired "spies" (disguised as laborers) who reported to management improper behavior in the workplace or union activity. Officials lobbied for keeping taxes low and making sure community development (like road building) benefited company operations. Without any judicial or law enforcement officials on site, company supervisory personnel were called on in emergency situations to take action, such as when a "love triangle" ended up with the death of a boyfriend.

Rose Fish recalled working in the flooring plant with nine other women who were in their late teens or early twenties. They stacked and sorted lumber that was between two and sixteen feet in length. Payment was in paper coupons that could be cashed at the store. Her parents paid six dollars per month for rent, and they later bought the house. At the same time, her mother took in a boarder who paid thirty dollars per month for room and board. When asked about attitudes toward the company, she said, "They were the cheapest town in the world." Consensus seems to have been that owners were, at best, respected or tolerated. Acceptance of the disparity in wealth between the Earles and townsfolk grew thin over the years.

Initially, base wages for general laborers were one dollar per day, with a six-day week. Frank Kobasic worked for IXL in the 1940s and recalled working for thirty-seven and a half cents per hour and a six-day, forty-hour week. Employees were charged for rent, fuel, ice, pasturage for livestock and store purchases. The company store delivered grocery orders that were submitted. Its merchandise selection was highly varied, from groceries to hardware and firearms to farm implements. In addition, employees paid 2 percent of their wages for physician coverage and for up to a week of sick time. Frequently, life insurance was provided by the fraternal organizations. House maintenance was performed by the company, such as annual cleaning or repair of a chimney or providing white paint for the exterior. One unique practice was the provision of Christmas presents from the company for the employees' children. Schoolteachers were enlisted to provide guidance to Dr. Earle's wife, who made an annual pilgrimage to Marshall Field's in Chicago to procure the yuletide gifts. Other former employees have no recollection of this practice, so it may not have been universal over time.

Dan O'Donnell recalled his grandfather's stories of the company's efforts to discourage union organizing. Despite its best efforts, there was a three-week strike in early 1920. Before the strike, IXL was paying $2.50 per day, whereas the I. Stephenson Company was paying $4.00. Earle argued that Hermansville employees didn't have to pay for a streetcar ride to and from work and had low housing costs. In the end, he agreed to a $0.50 raise and a nine-hour day, down from the previous ten-hour day. During the Depression, work hours were parceled out so each man got some work, and salaried compensation was reduced across the board.

Some of the town's character was influenced by its small-town, rural nature or the presence of a major factory. Garbage not taken to the dump meant bears in the backyard. Outhouses needed to be reinforced so they didn't get tipped over by teenagers. The mill whistles would punctuate the constant drone of the saws and other machinery from the mill, although Meyer had intentionally tried to segregate the industrial and residential areas of the town when it was initially laid out. Chewing tobacco took precedence over smoking due to the prohibition of its use around sawdust and wood shavings around the mill. Even so, the town had at least fifteen substantial fires. Partial explanation for the fires can be found in one humorous story. When a visitor wanted to light up his pipe, a resident said, "No problem," as there was enough hot ash in the air to ignite the tobacco. Clearly the wood-burning boilers for the steam-powered machinery had a downside. The mix

IXL coinage could be redeemed at community stores and neighboring regions. *IXL Historical Museum.*

of foreign languages sometimes led to comical exchanges in the stores when customers had to "act out" the use of an item to communicate what they wanted. One odd practice was that parishioners paid a twenty-five-cent fee for the use of a pew section—certainly more a function of the times than of the company town.

After leading Wisconsin Land and Lumber (more frequently referred to as IXL) from near financial collapse, Dr. Earle died in 1923. His sons, Harold and Stewart, took over company leadership until it was sold to Furblo (a heating and ventilating metal industry firm). Along the way, a lumber mill in LaBranche had been purchased, along with similar operations in Blaney Park and Simmons (near Gould City). IXL's competitive edge had been lost. Electric sanding machines had diminished its advantage. The major cutover landownership became a significant tax burden. Its investment value did not materialize, as the landscape was littered with stumps and not deemed soil-rich enough for farming. IXL employees had dipped from 350 in 1923 to 85 in 1943. In 1964, IXL ceased operations after eighty-six years at Hermansville. In 1957, a Citizens Improvement Association was developed to foster community development. Houses were sold to occupants for $600 each.

Hermansville in 2014 is a village with a post office, a senior center ("Community Club"), an American Legion post and hall, a library, the Wildwood restaurant, a gas station, auto repair and service, a bar (Broad Axe Saloon), fire and emergency services, several small industrial shops, hair salons, two baseball fields, a golf course, two churches, an elementary school and forestry-related businesses. There are two museums: the Vietnam War Museum and the IXL Historical Museum, focused on the history of the Wisconsin Land and Lumber Company. The Wisconsin Land and Lumber Company Office Building (located on museum grounds) is on the National Register of Historic Places.

NAHMA

Located on the north shore of Lake Michigan between the Garden peninsula and the Stonington peninsula, as well as between Garden and Rapid River, is a short point separating Ogontz Bay from the larger Big Bay De Noc. This ready access to deep water was an attractive feature for large-ship navigation. The river mouth area was identified in the 1836 Treaty of Washington as a reservation site for Native Americans. The district was called Nahma from the time of its earliest inhabitants, the Ojibwa, Ottawa and Potawatomi Native Americans. Their Anishinaabe-language word for sturgeon is pronounced "nahma." The river that empties into Lake Michigan at this point was once plentiful with sturgeon. The common contemporary pronunciation is with the first *a* long and the accent on the first syllable. The accurate Anishinaabe pronunciation has the first *a* as a short *e* and the second *a* long, with the accent on the second syllable.

Oral tradition has it that the Native Americans migrated from the easterly nearby Garden peninsula, after originating from farther eastern areas such as Sault Ste. Marie, Drummond and Sugar Islands. Evidence of the Native American community in the area includes arrowheads and Indian trails leading in a northern direction toward Lake Superior and in an easterly direction toward Manistique. The earliest residents appear to have been seasonally migratory; later, permanent settlements were focused at the mouth of the river and an area three miles west, now called "Indian Point." Their lifestyle was initially characterized by hunting, fishing and basket making (using porcupine quills) and then later by trapping and, even later, by logging and millwork. Their diet was based on venison, beaver and fish and enhanced with wild blueberries, raspberries, blackberries and cranberries. The term "nahma" was mentioned several times in Henry Wadsworth Longfellow's poem *The Song of Hiawatha* in 1855, as a reference to the sturgeon. The large sturgeon and its oil had a position of prominence in the Native American worldview. In the poem, the fish's oil is given special attributes and brings Hiawatha good fortune.

The first inhabitants of European descent were drawn by the first sawmill in 1848, which was located just north of the current village of Nahma and operated by George Richards and S.W. Kerfoot. It operated by water power until replaced later by the use of steam power. Ownership of this and another earlier sawmill changed hands several times until the land was purchased by the Oconto Company in 1881.

Located in Oconto, Wisconsin, eighty miles to the south, the Oconto Company found that its supply of logs was not meeting the needs of its customers. Its president, George Farnsworth, was the son of a fur trader, William, and a trading post owner, "Queen Marinette," namesake of Marinette, Wisconsin. After completing his purchase of 125 acres in what had once been part of the Wisconsin Territory, he loaded up two oxen, a team of horses, equipment, supplies and sixty men on a scow and headed out of Green Bay and into northern Lake Michigan. When he arrived, the

The planing mill frequently accompanied the shingle mill at large lumber mill sites. *Delta County Historical Museum.*

Native Americans at St. Lawrence Catholic Church with the Jesuit priest. *Delta County Historical Museum.*

animals had to swim ashore, and the supplies and equipment needed to be rafted to firm ground. But by 1856, the growing population had led to the establishment of the first Nahma post office. When Delta County was established in 1862, there were only two townships in the county: Escanaba and Nahma.

Michigan law required a separate corporate entity from the Oconto Company, so the Bay de Noquet Company was founded in 1881, its name taken from the Noquet tribe of Native Americans. George's son, G.J. Farnsworth, replaced him as president until his own replacement by Charles Good. The company's assets expanded to include 200,000 acres north from Nahma to within seven miles of Lake Superior. A maximum number employed at the mill in Nahma and in the lumber camps is estimated to have reached 1,200. Annual output of lumber reached 25 million board feet. The primary distribution method of shipping lumber, cedar posts, telephone poles and shingles was with large barges and tugboats. Some, however, left on the Soo Line railroad that ran in an east–west direction, and some left on steamboats. The company had a major harbor, with a twelve-foot draft and three docks. Lumber was shipped to locales in southern Michigan, Illinois, Ohio and New York. The daily activity included as much as half a dozen boatloads.

Initially, logs were floated down the Sturgeon River from the logging camps in the north. When the supply of lighter pines (white and Norway)

The Nahma company store's inventory ranged from groceries to hardware and yard goods. Weekly orders were delivered to area homes. *Delta County Historical Museum.*

was exhausted and replaced with the heavier hardwoods, another method of transport was needed. In 1902, a railroad was constructed to ship hardwood logs from the camps to the mill. The Nahma and Northern railroad included sixty-five miles of track, four locomotives and one hundred cars. This was not a narrow-gauge railroad, found in many logging operations, but rather a normal-gauge track. Typically, two trainloads of logs arrived daily in Nahma from the logging camps. The steel rails used had been discarded by the Soo Line after use in its system. Because so little underpinning went into rail beds for the Nahma and Northern tracks, the primary season for use of the line was in the winter, when the ground was frozen.

In addition to lumber, output from the mill included cedar posts, telephone poles, railroad ties, shingles and excelsior, wood strips used as packing material. When the prime soft and hardwoods had been harvested, pulpwood was cut and shipped for use in paper mills or for wood alcohol in chemical companies. A wide variety of nationalities was represented in local residents: French, Bohemian, Swedish, Norwegian, German, Polish and Czech.

The mill depended on four to six logging camps to supply timber for the lumber and related production. About half of the camps were owned and operated by the company and utilized thirty to forty men per camp. There were also independent or "jobber" camps that were allowed to cut timber on Bay de Noquet–owned land for sale to the company. Some of that timber went to firms other than Bay de Noquet, such as the paper mill in Escanaba and the chemical plant in Gladstone. Some of the camps took on a unique character. The Moses Camp had all Native American workers, another was composed primarily of Finnish employees and in another half were recent Russian immigrants; during World War II, one used German prisoners of war. Of course, the Finnish camps included an additional building, a sauna; in addition, Finnish camps were more likely to have the loggers' entire families on-site. Camp rates of pay in the 1940s ranged from $45 per month base pay to $60 for a teamster. A productive piece-worker could make $120—all of these included room and board. Much of the cutting was done during the winter months. The frozen ground made movement of the fallen trees easier. When the Sturgeon River was used, logs were stacked near the river, and a "drive" was conducted during the spring breakup. The camps remained in contact with the company through telephone lines. With no telephone poles, the lines were simply attached to or draped over tree limbs.

All indications are that these camps were demanding on the workers. Men slept two to a bunk, and lice, ticks and mosquitoes were thick. Kerosene was mixed with grease to ward off critters, as were fresh cedar boughs in the bedding. One observer was surprised to see the popularity of fine pocket watches as purchases for loggers. After all, when the work schedule was from dawn to dusk, what difference did the time make? Later discovery revealed that they played a critical role for pawning during "downtime" for the logger.

The town of Nahma included more than one hundred residential homes, a general store, a hotel, a boardinghouse (eighty beds), a dining hall, a post office, a small hospital, a maternity house, two churches, a gymnasium/auditorium, an airport, tennis courts, a golf course, a public beach and, the highlight, a community center (the "Club House"), which was the social center of the community. The Club House—which included a bar, men's and women's lounges, a soda fountain, a barbershop, a library, a gymnasium/auditorium, bowling lanes and a candy counter—hosted ladies' card parties in the afternoons and American Legion meetings in the evenings. Of course, this was in addition to business-related structures, such as an office building, a sawmill, a roundhouse, two power plants, lumberyards for storage and shipping, large tramways, a horse barn, planing and shingle mills, storage sheds and a silo-like sawdust and scrap burner. Adjacent to the town but across the river was Sandtown, a Native American community. The other end of town, on the east, was called "Fish Town."

As a company town, houses were rented to employees for seven to twelve dollars per month, and the general store had a monopoly on retail activity. The company doctor provided medical care to residents for a two-dollar monthly fee. As the landlord, the company took care of house maintenance, repairing the roof and providing paint. For a relatively small fee, loads of firewood were delivered for heating and cooking. When an employee retired or died, he or his surviving spouse was allowed to remain living in the house. When employees needed merchandise from the store or other services, charges were tallied, processed and paid once a month. Such charges would be items from camp stores, the Club House, rent or the monthly fee for medical services. Employees (or, more likely, their wives) typically checked the company office once a week to see their balances. Very few women worked outside the home, other than schoolteachers or a few secretarial or clerical workers in the office. During World War II, many women took the places of those male

The Nahma mill was battered by a Lake Michigan storm. The elevated tramway, common to many mills, is evident. *Delta County Historical Museum.*

millworkers who had left for military service. Standard procedure was for residents to submit a grocery order once a week, and it would later be delivered to their homes. The company's major wholesale supplier for store goods was a firm located in the Menominee/Marinette area.

Employees were allowed to "go in the red" with their charges at the store. The general store had to stock an extensive collection of items, as it was the complete source of shopping for residents—not only groceries and first aid supplies but also hardware, housewares, toiletries, men's and women's clothing and even window pane glass. Pharmaceuticals were dispensed through the hospital.

In general, residents seem to have been satisfied with the "company town" structure to their community. One woman interviewed said, "It was like everything was ours, but nothing was ours." Although the company store was "the only game in town," residents did make purchases in neighboring towns of Ensign and Isabella or through mail order with Sears or from traveling salesmen, such as Jewel Tea.

Fires plagued the town throughout Nahma's history. These affected the mill operation, as in 1899, as well as fifteen homes and industrial buildings in 1923. The latter event resulted in a conversion to an all-electric mill, one of the first and largest in the Midwest. In 1899, when the mill itself burned, equipment was removed from a recently defunct mill in Manistique, more than one hundred nautical miles away, and put in operation at the Nahma site in short order.

Expressions of faith took many forms in the community. Native Americans had settled near the mouth of the Sturgeon River and a location three miles to the west, now called Indian Point, at the edge of Ogonz Bay. This became the location of a Jesuit mission church in 1882, St. Lawrence Catholic Church, which served the primarily Native American community in the area until it was closed in the 1960s. Services were conducted in the Anishinaabe language and included Anishinaabe-language songbooks. The site also includes a Native American cemetery. In 1904, a Union church was constructed to accommodate a variety of backgrounds and traditions. In the 1950s, it was deeded to the Episcopal diocese by Warren Miller and named St. Paul's. It frequently went by the name of "the little brown church" and as of 2014 houses the Nahma Township Historical Museum. In 1905, St. Andrews Catholic Church was constructed in town and still serves the community. In 1906, Bethany Lutheran Church was constructed in nearby Isabella. For the first twenty years, the primary language spoken in services there was Swedish.

The Nahma Club House attracted children and adults for a variety of activities, from viewing movies to bowling. *Delta County Historical Museum.*

Two school buildings were constructed by the company, along with a series of additions. Initially, there were several one-room schoolhouses, but as the population grew and a demand for higher grade levels increased, a second was needed for upper elementary, junior high and, finally, a high school. The high school, called the F.W. Good School, was named after the lumber company president's brother. It also served students from adjacent communities. One highlight was the basketball team's state championships in "Class E" for three years. For many years during the summer, Nahma hosted the Nahma Vacation School, also called the "Backwoods University." It was a two-week session for adults that featured distinguished professional and academic presenters. College faculty and professional artists and writers were brought in for instruction in writing and art classes such as painting and photography.

Other unique features of Nahma included an active commercial fishing activity that was independent of the Bay de Noquet lumber company. Its sales were focused in areas such as Milwaukee and Chicago. There were also a number of independent logging camps in the vicinity that were not owned by Bay de Noquet, but most sold primarily to Bay de Noquet. The company also sold ice harvested during the winter and stored in sawdust for use in iceboxes.

The Native American Sandtown community included twenty families. They paid one dollar per year in rent to the company for use of the land for their houses, which they themselves constructed. Many worked in the company wood yards or in the loading of the barges. For their work loading the ships, they were paid directly by the ship's captain: sixty-five cents per hour versus twenty-five cents for sorting lumber in the company lumberyard. Stories are told of Sandtown residents climbing trees to spot ships coming over the horizon. On the last shipment out of Nahma in 1951, the barge *Maitland* took 1.5 million board feet of pine and hardwood lumber to North Tonawanda, New York, for a furniture company.

The lifestyle of the Native Americans living in Sandtown was clearly below the standard for those residing in Nahma proper. Although they attended

Company president Charlie Good promotes the town sale at Nahma. *Delta County Historical Museum.*

the public schools and had full use of the Club House, where they attended movies and used the snack bar, other dimensions were clearly subpar. Their work in the mill was mostly confined to sorting and stacking lumber in the "yard." Their homes were tar paper shacks that had no chimneys (just holes in the roof), and a portion of their diet included discarded fish guts and unused portions (typically internal organs) from the slaughterhouse and butcher shop.

In the 1940s, it became apparent that the availability of timber for the Bay de Noquet Company was becoming limited. The company had purchased a large section of land from the Cleveland Cliffs Company near what became the Munising "Pictured Rocks" area on Lake Superior, eighty miles away. In addition, it later trucked logs from the Grand Marais area (nearly one hundred miles, one way). In October 1948, BDN stockholders were notified that it would be necessary to sell the company. Final approval followed in December. This information was not shared with the Nahma community. On February 1, 1951, the announcement was made that the Bay de Noquet Lumber Company was for sale at a price of $250,000. Much of the cutover land had been sold to the U.S. Forest Service for what became the Hiawatha National Forest. Other parcels were sold to paper companies, hunting clubs or private individuals. What was left was the village of Nahma and 4,300 acres between Lake Michigan and Highway U.S. 2. Many in Nahma were stunned. They were losing their major employer, their landlord and community leadership. Others felt that "they should have seen the handwriting on the wall" due to diminishing timber supply in the central Upper Peninsula. The company tried to soften the blow by setting aside $100,000 severance pay and seeking another employer for the community. A major marketing campaign was launched that included publicity that was truly national in focus.

The president, Charlie Good, launched a campaign that included bringing a railroad car of media personnel from Chicago to the U.P. It worked, as articles appeared in *Life* magazine and the *Wall Street Journal*. He received three hundred inquiries from around the country and some from overseas. His pledge was to sell only to a buyer who would fill the void as a major employer for the Nahma community. In September 1951, he found such a buyer: the American Playground Device Company of Anderson, Indiana. It was the major manufacturer of outdoor playground equipment in the United States.

American Playground immediately began work on modifying and restoring the industrial buildings to accommodate its needs. Its product lines, all of which needed wood products, included park, picnic, swimming pool and dressing room equipment, along with flagpoles and bicycle racks. Initially, it employed 50 employees (later rising to 100), quite short of the 250 who had been employed by Bay de Noquet at the time of the sale. American Playground's president, Warren Miller, also envisioned an expansion of the recreational opportunities at Nahma and hoped to attract other small employers to the area. Initial American Playground plans called for development of the Nahma area as a tourist and recreational area, including a new motel, a model playground and a logging museum, as well as upgrading the hotel and cottages.

Despite the best intentions of American Playground's president, the venture never prospered. In addition, the company was less enamored of the "company town" model. The physician moved to Manistique, and business in the store diminished as more residents, now owners of autos, chose to shop in Escanaba or Manistique. Residents were told to buy their houses or face the threat that someone else would buy them out from under them. A Community Coordinating Council was formed to foster community development. In 1970, Nahma's Good High School was sold, as the district had consolidated with others—such as nearby Fairbanks, Cooks and Garden—to form the Big Bay de Noc School District, located at Garden Corners.

When company leadership changed hands, the corporate interest in the Nahma area further diminished. Land that had been available for community use was sold to private owners, and in some cases, fees were instituted for services that had been free. The land occupied by Native Americans in Sandtown was sold, and they had to relocate. The corporate commitment to the Nahma community had diminished. American Playground vacated the area in the early 1990s. The township board began to play more of a leadership role in the community to fill the void left by a company.

Current activities in Nahma highlight a variety of recreational opportunities while celebrating its culture and history. Music festivals are held during the summer. Local businesses in 2014 include Christine's Gallery & Gifts, Nahma Golf Course (a nine-hole course and clubhouse), Nahma Inn & Arrow Lounge (including a restaurant) and the Upper Peninsula Golf & Lake Resort (including cabins and camping sites). In addition to the St. Andrews Catholic Church's activities are the Nahma Township Historical Society Museum and the DNR Boat Launch. A major current project is restoring the sawdust burner, which is on the National Register of Historic Places.

NEWBERRY

Located about halfway between Lake Superior and Lake Michigan in the eastern section of the Upper Peninsula, Newberry's blast furnace was heavily dependent on the development of the railroads, such as the Detroit, Mackinaw and Marquette. The surrounding forests provided a plentiful supply of logs for its lumber and charcoal/pig iron production facility that went by several names between 1882 and 1945: the Vulcan Furnace Company, Lake Superior Iron and Chemical Plant and the Newberry Lumber and Chemical Company. Other wood byproducts were also captured from the timber, such as wood alcohol.

As was common throughout the U.P., the lumber mill at Emerson had the silo-looking burner for sawdust and wood scraps. *Sterling McGuinn.*

Company houses in Newberry. *Sterling McGuinn.*

Vulcan Furnace Company constructed houses for its employees (evidence of such can be found on the north end of town) and a company store. Employee numbers rose to the five hundred to six hundred range. Iron ore came in on rail from the Marquette Range, was heated with locally produced charcoal and left by rail to Sault Ste. Marie, where it was shipped by vessel to steel mills. Limestone mined from the area was used in the furnaces, and the charcoal was heated in area kilns. The consumption of logs at the complex necessitated two narrow-gauge logging railroads to supply the kilns.

The Tahquamenon Logging Museum in Newberry has a wide variety of displays that illustrate the area's logging history and pig iron facility. Recent major employers included the state psychiatric hospital that is now closed and the current state correctional facility.

EMERSON

Emerson lies where the Tahquamenon River empties into Lake Superior's Whitefish Bay. The Cheesebrough Lumber Company constructed thirty houses and a store, along with a sawmill, a boardinghouse, a blacksmith shop, a school and a company office. The mill operated from 1882 until 1912, shipping lumber to Chicago and New York State. Ojibwas from the Bay Mills community, fifteen miles to the north, assisted in the loading of ships at Emerson.

Emerson buildings in the 1890s: the owner's cottage, the Emerson Inn and a store. *Sterling McGinn.*

SHELLDRAKE

Located eight miles south of Whitefish Point, which protrudes into eastern Lake Superior and forms Whitefish Bay, Shelldrake takes its name from an Ojibwa word for a type of duck that frequented the area. Originally a Native American fishing village, the Moore, Park & Sharpe Lumber Company established what was a model town for its day in 1895. A hotel, a general store, a hospital, a school, a clubhouse, a boardinghouse, an icehouse and a long boardwalk were constructed, along with the lumber mill, elevated tramway and associated industrial facilities such as a blacksmith shop and barns. Residential buildings had plastered walls and running hot water, quite unusual for that era, especially in lumber towns. The store stocked groceries, yard goods and feed and grain. The boardinghouse was named the Bay City House, after Bay City, Michigan, home of the new owners, the Penoyer brothers.

The mill continued to thrive, employing up to nine hundred employees, utilizing twelve logging camps and adding a logging railroad. Forests provided hemlock, spruce, ironwood and other hardwoods as Calumet and Hecla of Keweenaw and the Bartlett Lumber Company succeeded the Penoyers. Church services were held in the school. The clubhouse was the entertainment center for the region, drawing visitors from other communities. Similar trips were made to Shelldrake for supplies in the general store or the medical services of the physician. Commercial fishing also was successful with the Brown Fisheries in Shelldrake.

The town had fire hydrants for protection, but two major fires caused heavy damage, the second of which, in 1925, marked the end of the mill

The Shelldrake lumber mill had the raised trams for transport of lumber and logs. *John M. Longyear Research Library.*

and, eventually, the town. The current status of Shelldrake can best be indicated by the primary sources for the information provided: two volumes by Larry Wakefield and Roy Dodge, both on Michigan ghost towns. Only a historical marker designates the location along the highway, once a major logging producer, despite a few attempts to revive the area as a resort facility.

BLANEY

A rough-and-tumble logging camp was transformed into a model logging village and then an exclusive resort in the midst of the northern wilderness. The community of Blaney, later renamed Blaney Park, is situated more than twenty miles northeast of Manistique and lies ten miles north of Lake Michigan. In 1898, the MacEachern Lumber Company sold its Blaney area landholdings to William Mueller of Chicago. Mueller was a former machinist who repaired railroad cars and became a major ship owner on the Great Lakes. He was determined to establish a new model for a modern lumber company, distinct from the sordid camps and communities common across the peninsula. He had cottages built in an orderly pattern that more closely resembled a modern town of its time than a shantytown, with the typical tar paper shacks found in many logging communities. Also constructed were a large boardinghouse and a company store that boasted of its vast inventory.

Included in the revamped community were a large storehouse of feed and grain to supply the company's horses and oxen, a blacksmith shop, a machine shop, a roundhouse, a depot and a large, substantial home for Mr. Mueller. The sixteen cottages were for department heads in the mill town. General millworkers lived in the "Saginaw district" adjacent to the mill. There were sixteen logging camps that supported the two mills, one lumber and one shingle. The town's name came from the captain of one of Mueller's ships that hauled cedar products from Manistique to Chicago. Captain Neal Blaney was of Irish background and left his seafaring duties for a while to help start up and manage the Blaney operation along with the owner's son, William Mueller Jr., who did much of the design work for the Blaney town. The Blaney and Southern Railroad was established and equipped with engines and rail cars. It connected the mills at Blaney with the east–west Soo Line railroad and the area's logging camps. The rail connection with the Soo Line became known as the Blaney Junction and facilitated the route to Manistique, where most of the Blaney logs left by ship. The primary finished products were cedar: telephone and telegraph posts, railroad ties and shingles. The town did have a tavern, but beer and liquor sales were restricted to those who had the permission of the company physician. Evening hours were limited, and Sunday hours were nonexistent. Mueller's forestlands stretched forty miles north to Lake Superior and ten miles south to Lake Michigan.

After the turn of the century, Mueller suffered a series of financial difficulties (as did many in the country). He borrowed heavily from Dr. George Earle, owner of the Wisconsin Land and Lumber (IXL) in Hermansville. His first attempt to complete a sale to Wisconsin Land and Lumber was unsuccessful, but it was finally consummated in the 1907–9 period. The backstory was that the Blaney operation owed Wisconsin Land and Lumber $98,000, and its Chicago bankers were increasingly uncomfortable with Mueller's debt load. Dr. Earle was keenly interested in the hardwoods that Mueller had ignored on his holdings. Wisconsin Land and Lumber logged at Blaney for sixteen years, so it was a major supplier of logs for IXL. In addition to more than 50 million board feet of hardwoods, they harvested cedar and pulpwood.

By 1927, the Blaney holdings had been substantially logged of their valuable timber. Dr. Earle had died, and his sons, Stewart and Harold, had succeeded him in the company's leadership. They were interested in finding another use for cutover land. Considerable acreage was being turned over to the state as a method of addressing delinquent taxes. This was a major issue across the peninsula, as it was discovered that the soil (contrary to the assumption of many), along with a short growing season, was not especially valuable for most agricultural purposes. A 1920 arrangement with some cattlemen from the West brought 2,500 head of two-year-old western steers in to be fattened up on the cleared land. The Blaney, Land & Cattle Company was formed, and feeding sheds were built. The venture failed, and half the herd was sent back to the Green Bay area for "reconditioning." Other ventures included harvesting cordwood for charcoal production to be used in pig iron furnaces at Newberry and the import of twenty families from Kentucky to work in the north woods. After this series of dead-ends, the Earle brothers assessed

Modernizing at Blaney meant tractors replacing horses, mules and oxen in log transport. *IXL Historical Museum.*

their land assets at Blaney and decided on establishing a major recreational center, which soon became the new mission for Blaney, as it was transformed into Blaney Park.

Blaney Park Resort was to become a forest preserve and recreational center utilizing the lakes, streams, wildlife and forests. Cottages were refurbished, modern plumbing connected, a swimming pool dug, a nine-hole golf course established, an archery range erected, an airport implemented and the boardinghouse transformed into a hotel. The thirty-five- by seventy-foot pool featured both a low and high diving board and underwater lighting, an unusual feature for the time. Additional recreational options included a shuffleboard court, horseshoe pits and tennis courts. Young children enjoyed ponies, a playground and a wading pool. In the hopes of attracting the financially affluent, finishing and furnishings were upgraded, such as with wicker furniture. Cottages were established at three area lakes (Ford Lake, Tee Lake and Lake Anne Louise) for those who didn't want to stay at the hotel. Lake Anne Louise (named for one of Harold Earle's daughters) was created through a sixty-acre excavation and damming project. All meals were served at the hotel, although some cottages were equipped with stoves for "housekeeping" if guests preferred to cook their own meals. The former boardinghouse was transformed into an upscale hotel and dining area, while the former Mueller home became the exclusive lodging facility called Celibeth House (so named from the combination of two Earle cousins, Celila and Elizabeth). Dinner guests could enjoy orchestra music while dining and stay for dancing if they wished.

Nine ranger stations were established to monitor forest fires, and fire towers were erected along with beefed-up firefighting equipment and services. Partnerships were developed with state and federal wildlife agencies to develop and restock inland fisheries. Architects, engineers and landscape professionals were brought in for design guidance. An ornithologist was hired to oversee wildlife development, study it and educate visitors, who included naturalists as well as tourists. A talented storyteller, Dr. Karl Christofferson, lived in a small cottage on the grounds for years and is reported to have banded more than thirty thousand birds and identified 207 species. Banded birds led to reports being sent back from Greenland. Species were protected from hunters and poachers so that beaver, muskrat, otters and mink could flourish. Fishing enthusiasts caught bass, pike and trout. There were seventy miles of fencing erected and fifty miles of roads improved to support fire lanes, hiking and horseback

Some of the facilities at Blaney Park under Earle ownership were modern. *IXL Historical Museum.*

riding. Seventy skilled tradesmen were brought over from Hermansville for weeklong assignments in Blaney's retrofit.

Deer hunting was allowed only during the fall seasons (archery and rifle) and limited to one-third of the twenty-two thousand acres. Trapping could be done only by the rangers, who focused on limiting the number of predatory coyotes and opossum, labeled as vermin, so other species could flourish. The Blaney Park facilities were enhanced by the Earle acquisition of nearby Simmons Woods area, which added Lake Michigan beaches to the resort's portfolio. Simmons was available for day trips from Blaney Park for those who wanted to explore further. Boats were provided for use at Blaney or Simmons. The Paul Bunyan theme was used throughout the Blaney resort. The former schoolhouse was now the Paul Bunyan Playhouse and also hosted movies and church services. The logging exhibits in the Paul Bunyan Museum included oversized tools presented as Paul's. The IXL logo was enhanced with Paul's face for the resort. "Paul Bunyan's Store" was a general store and also provided souvenirs and sporting goods for tourists. The resort flourished for thirty-five years and could accommodate 250 guests at a time.

After the closing of the resort, the land was sold off to a number of private owners or became part of state or federal recreational areas. Tourism is still a common theme in the area, with a bed-and-breakfast in the former Celibeth House, an antique shop in the former playhouse and a restaurant in the former hotel. Also surviving is "Park" as part of the full name for Blaney.

SAULT STE. MARIE

Although it could hardly be called a company town, Sault Ste. Marie's major employer, Northwestern Leather Company, certainly exhibited some features commonly found in a company town. The tannery constructed houses for its employees in a neighborhood on the west edge of town called "Algonquin." Employees normally rented the houses, but many ended up purchasing them; it was also common to have their purchased houses moved to another location in the community. The Tannery Clubhouse was constructed and functioned as a recreation center. Ping-pong, badminton, boxing, wrestling and basketball events occurred there. The company sponsored basketball, softball and hockey teams, the latter competing in the Industrial Hockey League. With other major employers in town like Union Carbide, a woolen mill and lumber mills, the local economy was diversified.

The location of the factory on the edge of town prompted the streetcar line to make a tailored run in its schedule for the tannery employees, a workforce that rose to about nine hundred strong. Hemlock bark from regional forests was ground up for treating hides that arrived from around the United States and even Sweden and Australia. A major product from the plant was shoe leather for the upper section of the shoe or boot. Employees stripped hides of any remaining animal tissues and then processed the leather with pasting, shaving and buffing machines. The Northwestern Leather Company, which operated from 1900 until 1958, received its greatest fame when it and its employees received the Army-Navy "E" Award for the quality of military

The Northwestern Tannery at Sault Ste. Marie constructed homes for its employees and also a community center. *Chippewa County Historical Society.*

boots produced during World War II. Its darkest hour was likely in 1980, when the Environmental Protection Agency (EPA) validated toxins at the former site, necessitating major environmental cleanup activity. Little evidence of the tannery remains today, but Sault Ste. Marie is a thriving community of fourteen thousand.

SIMMONS

Roughly halfway between Manistique and St. Ignace and seven miles south of Gould City lies the former hamlet of Simmons. On the shores of the small inland Duel Lake, what was later called Simmons Woods was only a mile north of the northern shore of Lake Michigan. Simmons took its name from the Simmons Furniture Company, located in Kenosha in southern Wisconsin, which used hardwood lumber in framing its bedding products. Early records indicate that the region was first occupied by Native Americans, who were located in the adjacent Fox Point area on Lake Michigan. In 1868, the first settlers of European background arrived there, as well as in the Scott Point area five miles west, also on Lake Michigan. Both groups' livelihoods were based on fishing, hunting and trapping. The first Europeans were primarily from Canada or other parts of the United States, with few recent immigrants. Recorded names indicate a strong presence of French nationality. Initially, they spent their winter seasons on Mackinaw Island, until logging activities proved productive. Legend has it that the first area mail service was provided by a local Native American, "Alex." He traversed the twice-weekly routes from Naubinway to St. Ignace on foot for many years, a ninety-mile round-trip jaunt.

The Newton Brothers Fish Company was a thriving business and shipped its salted fish eastward to St. Ignace or westerly to Manistique on small steamers. The company constructed docks to accommodate the ships. Coopers were employed to manufacture barrels from area ash forests to pack the fish. The soon-defunct community near Scott Point was called Orville and had a school and a post office. The area township in Mackinaw County is called Newton Township. Area Native Americans began harvesting wide slabs of cedar bark and log to be used for roofing. These were bartered for food or other goods such as blankets. Soon logging camps popped up in the area along with the establishment of the Don Ross Lumber Company. Such development was spurred along by the initiation of the Minneapolis, St. Paul and Sault Ste. Marie Railroad line through the area with a station near Gould City in 1897. In addition to turning out telegraph posts, Ross Lumber manufactured an interesting product for the growing country's city streets. These were short cedar posts, one foot in length, stood on end to create a street surface. The timber industry's growth prompted a land speculator, Fred Cooper, to begin buying up land in the area. He sold his holdings to the Simmons Company in 1902.

Simmons's personnel soon began erecting buildings on the southern, northern and eastern sides of Duel Lake. Lumber and shingle mills were accompanied by dry kilns, barns, a blacksmith shop, a locomotive shed, an office and a store. A boardinghouse, workers' homes, a town hall, a schoolhouse and a clubhouse were also included. A slaughterhouse was constructed away from the settlement, and there were a number of small, one-person shacks nearby. These were merely for sleeping, as laborers obtained their meals from the boardinghouse. The houses and cottages were made of rough lumber, with little "finishing" on either the interior or exterior walls. The Simmons and Northern Railroad was established. It brought logs from the camps to the mills and then transported lumber products to the Minneapolis, St. Paul and Sault Ste. Marie (later called the Soo Line, a subsidiary of the Canadian National rail company) rail connection at a site called Bovee near Gould City. Job titles provide a flavor of the community: millworker, engineer, teamster, cook, wash lady, blacksmith, millwright, carpenter, barn boss, lumber piler and lumber scaler.

Church services were held occasionally in either the school or town hall, but not on a regular schedule. Dances and socials, or an occasional school program, also brought area residents together. The primary recreational activity seems to have been focused around the town's baseball team. The on-site mill manager was a former college baseball player. Allegedly, he recruited former team members to work in Simmons as a way of strengthening his team. They established an excellent record and played teams from Blaney, Gladstone, Escanaba, Hermansville, Newberry and Sault Ste. Marie. One year, when they had an especially talented team, they went as far as the Keweenaw Peninsula for games.

Less successful were his plans for expanding the town's economy beyond lumber production. One plan, dropped after one attempt, was to dry wild berries and fruit from the area and use them the following winter. His second plan had preliminary success: manufacturing maple syrup without using maple sap. Instead, he cooked pieces of maple wood along with plenty of brown sugar. Its success was terminated when federal food labeling laws required a list of ingredients. A frequently told story about mill life has to do with one of the mules that was used for transport of lumber around the mill yard. When the mill whistle would blow at the end of the day's shift, he would literally stop still in his tracks, unwilling to pull any more that day.

When the Simmons Furniture Company discovered the advantage of using steel in its bed frames, the need for northern Michigan hardwoods evaporated. The town was sold to the Earle Lumber Company of Hermansville (IXL/Wisconsin Land and Lumber) in 1907. It ran the mill for one year and then sent the logs by rail to Hermansville for milling. Later, when Wisconsin Land and Lumber developed Blaney Park as a recreational facility (thirty miles to the northwest), Simmons Woods (also called Simmon's Wood) was utilized for day trips for tourists staying at Blaney. They came to Simmons to hike, fish and explore the natural surroundings. The Simmons area has quite a diverse collection of tree species, including spruce, balsam, birch, poplar, beech, elm and basswood.

In 1968, the land was sold to Bethlehem Steel, which was hoping to utilize the limestone for its steel manufacturing. For many years, it employed a caretaker who facilitated and oversaw recreational use of the property for hunting, fishing and camping. When the limestone quarry never materialized (rumors circulated that it was under consideration as a site for a nuclear power plant), it was acquired by the Michigan Nature Conservatory in May 1995. The conservatory held it for purchase by the State of Michigan, which established the area as part of the Lake Superior State Forest. At ten thousand acres, it was the largest such venture of the conservatory to date; it was named the Crow River project. A township park is located on Lake Michigan near the former site of Orville at Scott Point. The former Simmons town site and Duel Lake are contained in the Lake Superior State Forest.

FIBORN

Not all mining in the Upper Peninsula was focused on the pursuit of copper and iron, or even silver or gold. Limestone quarries popped up all across the peninsula, as limestone was desirable for its function as a purifier in the iron-making process. Limestone extraction facilities are still thriving industries along the southern Lake Michigan shore in places like Gulliver (Port Inland), Cedarville and Drummond Island. Located (roughly) between Rexton and Trout Lake, and north of Epoufette, Fiborn's caves, sinkholes and limestone were first highlighted by a surveyor, Henry Brevoort, in 1845 in what is now Hendricks Township in Mackinaw County. It was Michigan's future governor Charles Osborn who initiated the first mining operation with William Fitch, president of the Duluth, South Shore and Atlantic Railroad; they combined their names to create "Fiborn." This was truly an undeveloped wilderness area, accessible only by railroad for many years. This was not "just another quarry." What became an identifiable name, Fiborn limestone, was notable for its uniquely high calcium and low magnesium content.

Activities at Fiborn were focused on the mining (with the use of dynamite and steam shovel), crushing and shipping of the rock. Other than steelmaking, some was used for calcium carbide manufacture and some road building. Initial buildings in 1905 that followed the arrival of the new three-mile rail spur connecting with the main line of the Duluth, South Shore and Atlantic railroad were the three-story boardinghouse and, later, the company store that included a post office. Additional

This equipment at the Hendricks Quarry was the same type used at the neighboring Fiborn Quarry. *Sterling McGinn.*

industrial development included locomotive sheds, a crusher and a large steam shovel that operated on rails and, later, a magazine for the dynamite storage. Railroads played a key role for Fiborn. Locomotives and cars were essential for movement of crushed rock within the quarry area and for transport to the main rail line to the north. Smaller engines, called "dinkeys," were used around the quarry area.

The boardinghouse provided sleeping facilities and meals for the male mining workforce. It also functioned as a hotel, and the open section on the first floor served as a social gathering place for dances, traveling salesmen's presentations and worship services conducted by itinerant clergy. Five women worked in the boardinghouse providing housekeeping, cooking or waitstaff service. Residents of Fiborn represented a wide variety of European ethnic backgrounds and a mixture of immigrants and those born in the United States. Recreational activities included baseball, swimming and skating. Some families grew vegetable gardens for their own use, and hunting and trapping were also common for supplementing diet or income. The cool caves were sometimes used for preserving food. Available information on the life of Fiborn was very limited, and before the publishing of Mark Whitney's thorough and detailed *Fiborn Quarry: Then and Now* in 2014, it was limited to local stories and the Michigan Karst Conservatory website (caves.org/conservancy/mkc). Initially, the only private homes were five block houses constructed for managers and supervisors by the company. Later, individuals who wanted to have their families join them constructed wooden-frame homes nearby. The only other non-industrial building to appear was a stone school facility.

The one-room schoolhouse operated from 1907 until the 1930s. In 1911, there were sixteen pupils, five school board members and a teacher, Florence Cheeseman, listed in the year's commemorative program. The highest grade was the eighth. By 1927, there were seventy-five local residents identified. In 1930, there were forty-three employed at the quarry. It's difficult to underestimate the degree of isolation that folks at Fiborn experienced. For social contacts outside the community, their options were either hopping a train thirty miles to Newberry or St. Ignace or walking five miles to Trout Lake or Rexton. The first road for automotive travel did not appear until 1916. By 1930, fifteen families were living in separate homes, and only six individuals lived in the boardinghouse.

In 1909, ownership of Fiborn passed from Fitch and Osborn to one of their primary customers, the Algoma Steel Company, located at Sault Ste. Marie, Ontario. The company continued to operate it for its steel production, especially the manufacture of rail tracks for trains. By 1936, Algoma had discovered a less expensive source for limestone in Rogers City, located fifty miles south of the Mackinaw straits on Lake Huron. The Fiborn facility remained idle, and many folks moved away or found other area employment. For many years, its only use was for stone and gravel for area road development.

The Michigan Karst Conservatory took an interest in preserving the area for its unique geological features, such as the caves and other limestone formations. It purchased the area in 1987 from Algoma and established the Fiborn Karst Preserve. The conservatory has developed the area as a nature preserve with recreational hiking and conducts tours of the caves. Most of the surrounding area became part of Michigan's Lake Superior State Forest in the 1930s and is a popular recreational area. In 2014, the Graymont Mining Company approached the Michigan Department of Natural Resources about beginning limestone extraction operations on state lands in the adjacent Garfield Township. The Fiborn area's future looks very similar to its past—sparsely populated, with land use dependent on recreational use and possibly limestone extraction.

GOGEBIC COUNTY

The Gogebic Iron Range begins in Gogebic County at the far western end of the peninsula and was home to many mine sites, minimally developed locations and even some that rose to the status of towns and model towns. The first iron ore was shipped from the Colby Mine in 1884 on rail to Pennsylvania through Milwaukee. Arnold Alanen's fine discussion of community development in the area, *Homes on the Range*, identifies camps, unplotted or squatter's locations, along with locations as the primary settlements formed. Betty Sodders, who grew up in the area and has written extensively on Michigan history, agreed. Just across the state line, the Gogebic Iron Range included another twenty mines in Wisconsin, such as the surviving Montreal Mining Company Historic District in Montreal. The Michigan region has many towns and villages today that owe their origin to the iron mine ventures that would move from one section to another when the ore ran low.

Detailed records from the Oliver Iron Mining Company's Puritan mine reveal the nature of the company's maintenance of its employee housing. Approval from Duluth in 1926 included repair of windows, plumbing, foundations, chimneys, roofs, fences, woodsheds and sidewalks. Also included were interior and exterior painting, chimney inspection and cleaning and removal and installation of storm windows and screens. Expenditures per house for each service ranged from three to ten dollars per task per house.

The Asteroid and Plymouth Mines developed into full model towns, designed to attract and retain employees. The Asteroid was owned by the

Castile Mining Company and later combined with the Eureka Mine. It was a shaft facility and was located in the very small community of Ramsey, which had been the site of logging activity earlier. The mine began in 1906 and was located halfway between Wakefield and Bessemer. Ore was shipped on the Chicago and Northwestern Railroad to the northwest to Ashland, Wisconsin, where it went by freighter to steel mills in the southern Great Lakes. There were a number of single-family homes constructed by the company.

The Plymouth mine was located on Sandy Lake on the west side of Wakefield. It was an open-pit mine and operated between 1916 and 1952. Since the mines closed in the 1950s, the economy's focus has been on recreation and forestry-related activities. In 2014, exploratory drilling in northern Gogebic County gave hope for renewed mining activity, in this case copper, with the Highland Copper Company of Canada.

GWINN

Twenty miles directly south of Marquette on the north branch of the Escanaba River, William Gwinn Mather, president of the Cleveland Cliffs Iron Company (CCI), founded his model town of Gwinn in 1907. Several mines (many owned by CCI) and communities—Austin, Princeton, Stephenson and Smith—were already in the immediate area, adjacent to the 440-acre parcel of land that CCI purchased from the Chicago and North Western Railroad. These mines and their communities, along with others in the area such as New Swanzy, Swanzy and Little Lake, were growing at a rapid pace, and there was a need for houses, businesses and schools to support the employees.

Mather named the new community Gwinn, his mother's maiden name. Inspired by the design of some mining communities in Europe, he hired a well-known landscape architect, Warren H. Manning, from Boston to design his new model town. Model towns were a step up from the company towns of the era and certainly the mining "locations" so common throughout the Marquette Iron Range. Rather than a haphazard scattering of buildings typical of many locations, or even the monotonous uninspired sameness of many company towns, the model town was to provide an attractive and aesthetically pleasing appearance for its residents, distinct from the gritty surroundings of their workplaces.

Iron ore mining and related industries had begun in Marquette County in the 1840s. Actually, discoveries and development in the

The Cleveland Cliffs Hospital in Gwinn. *From Forsyth Township Historical Society.*

Gwinn district, also called the Swanzy District, of the Marquette Range occurred somewhat later (in the 1870s) than in many other areas such as Negaunee and Ishpeming, to the northwest. The Gwinn area Smith Mine, which later became the Cheshire and finally the Princeton, began in 1871. The newly acquired and developing mines prompted Cleveland Cliffs to act quickly with expanded facilities for its growing workforce and their families. The new homes had variety in structure, size and color. Significant attention was given to landscaping; one thousand new trees were planted, as were seventy-five shrubs, alongside many existing trees. An open park or "commons area" was created for public use, as was an attractive boulevard. Streets were wider than the norm, and other open or green areas were created throughout the community. The overall planning vision was that everyone would be within ten minutes of the surrounding area's natural beauty. CCI actually had a nursery to support its ongoing landscaping goals. Annual prizes were given to residents whose homes and grounds excelled in their appearance. Guidelines for homes insisted that any garage or small barn for a horse and cow had to be located behind the house. Pigsties were prohibited. Many homes had vegetable and flower gardens.

The Gwinn Clubhouse and community social center. *John M. Longyear Research Library.*

Landscaping, wide roads and fire hydrants were some key hallmarks of Gwinn's planned design. *John M. Longyear Research Library.*

Within two years, the flow of the river was altered, bridges constructed, water and sewer lines installed and roads graded. Diamond drilling beforehand had ruled out the later discovery of iron ore beneath the town that might require the shifting of any town buildings, an issue at other locations in the Marquette mining district. On the edge of town, at the fork of the middle branch and east branch of the Escanaba River, a canal was dug to limit potential damage to the town or mines from flooding. Estimates have between one hundred and two hundred workmen employed in the town's construction. Fifty-five company-owned homes were built and rented, many other lots sold for private construction (150 in the first few years) and thirty-one city blocks laid out. Most of the residential buildings were two-story duplexes called "double homes" at the time. Single-family homes were constructed for company management. Lots were also sold for private business, but the owners and the nature of the business had to pass muster with CCI. No houses of prostitution or bars were allowed, but one tavern was later tolerated as a method of controlling the flow of alcohol. If the company didn't approve of the potential business owner's character, the business was not approved. These attempts of social control were of limited success, as entrepreneurs could simply set up shop in a neighboring community. In addition, all businesses in the downtown section had to be constructed

Gwinn's older neighbor, Austin, had many company houses. *John M. Longyear Research Library.*

Like many of the era, Westman's Store in Republic was a community social center where folks chatted around the wood heater. *John M. Longyear Research Library.*

of brick for fire safety. Initial Gwinn businesses included a general store, and CCI constructed a hotel with twenty-five rooms and a dining room to accommodate sixty, the Gwinn Savings Bank and a hospital.

The Club House and its cost was a personal gift to the community by William Mather. With three floors plus a basement, it became the social and recreational center for the community. The nightly playing of films was a major portion of the community's social life, as audiences showed up to see the silent films of Chaplin, Valentino or Garbo, highlighted by the local piano player's enhancements and interpretations. Audiences of seventy or more enjoyed candy, soft drinks or the drinking fountain at intermission. Two smoke-filled bowling lanes somehow accommodated league players who used the two-hole balls. Meeting rooms were available for Boy Scouts and women's groups. The Club House also contained a gymnasium and a swimming pool, complete with lockers and showers. The gym supported gymnastic, boxing, weightlifting, wrestling and basketball activities. Other equipment included pool tables and a billiard table. Rooms were set aside for reading, and the library had more than one thousand books, eight newspapers and seventeen magazine subscriptions. Members paid fifty cents to join the Gwinn Association, which operated the Club House's programs that later included the activities at Bass Lake (just three miles away), which in turn operated a summer camp and recreation area. The association also hosted a community Christmas party.

The hospital served as the community doctor's office to address routine health issues as well as serious mine accidents. Hospital grounds included a barn equipped with buggy and sleigh for the doctor's home visits. The company physician was also surgeon and pharmacist. A visiting nurse program was later developed to provide in-home assistance tailored to the needs of women and children.

The first year, school classes had to be held on the second floor of one of the downtown business buildings. Soon a bond issue was passed, and a new school was in place. A high school building was soon to follow, also constructed via area taxpayers. Interestingly, female schoolteachers were expected to join the Women's Study Club, and they were restricted to one trip out of town per month. The surrounding area experienced considerable growth also, as CCI constructed (all in brick) a district office, central power plant, machine shops and a lab to support its several

Even these privies in Gwinn along this alley had a touch of elegance. *Forsyth Township Historical Society.*

mines. News reports of the day indicate that forest fires were a major problem and concern due to the hot sparks discharged from wood-burning locomotives. A new boardinghouse was constructed in Austin, in addition to the two already at Princeton. Little Lake, five miles east of Gwinn, was the area rail center for three companies, the Chicago and Northwestern, the Munising, Marquette and South East and the Duluth, Superior, Sault and Atlantic lines. Gwinn was connected with the Lake Superior and Ishpeming rail spur.

By 1911, surface workers at the mines were being paid $2.92 a day, while those who worked below the surface, in some cases six levels or four hundred feet below ground, received $2.62. Contract miners, who were paid either by how much ore they handled or the distance they progressed, averaged $2.72 a day. This was also the year the Western Federation Miners attempted to organize a union. The initial interest of three hundred at the first presentation had dwindled to twenty within a year.

A bandstand was erected in town, and the increased Gwinn Association Band grew to a membership of twenty-five. The most frequently identified nationalities in the area were Italian and Finnish. The number of churches also grew, including Finnish Lutheran, Catholic, Swedish Methodist, Episcopal and Mission.

What was initially called the "second Smith mine" (the first Smith mine was the predecessor to the early Princeton Mine adjacent to Gwinn) was renamed the Gwinn Mine and later the Archibald Mine. The Gwinn was joined by the Mackinaw, Gardner and Stephenson Mines as the more productive mines in the area; others included the Brotherton, Frances, Kidder and Cyr Mines. Gwinn functioned as the commercial center, as it was surrounded by mining communities. This continued until the Depression settled into the area and production fell off across the board. Some miners moved to the Negaunee/Ishpeming/North Lake area for more work. CCI allowed former employees to do mine maintenance in idle facilities or community work to help meet home rental obligations during lean times. Mather made personal contributions to the Club House and Gwinn Association during those Depression years. Surprisingly, the bank remained strong until it was sold to community members in the 1940s. CCI sold the Gwinn Mine in 1927, although its new owner enjoyed some productive years thereafter. In 1928, the hospital was closed. Records indicate that CCI had a very strong safety record in its Gwinn-area mines. The hotel

The store keeper and his family lived in this company home, although he was not a company employee. *From Forsyth Township Historical Society.*

closed in 1942, and the Club House was turned over to the school board in 1946. During World War II, the ore production at many mines rebounded significantly. In the years 1945–46, district mines produced 12 million tons of ore, but a major labor strike in 1948 coincided with the curtailment of mining activity in the area.

Mather's motivation in creating a model town was more than just filling a need for more roofs and beds for his miners. He wanted to attract and retain highly qualified and skilled employees. Experience had shown that married employees were less likely "move on" for any variety of reasons; therefore, simple boardinghouses would not do. In addition, benefits were seen as an antidote to labor militancy and unionism. CCI established a welfare department that oversaw pensions, safety, medical services and the Club House.

The Gwinn area experienced resurgence in 1955, when the KI Sawyer airport, five miles away, became a United States Air Force base. Home building increased dramatically in the area, commercial activity rebounded and enrollment in public schools soared. When the air force departed in 1994, the facility reverted to a county airport and business development zone. Employment opportunities for Gwinn's two thousand residents today are diversified between local retail or school, the nearby Sawyer complex or commuting to the mines or Marquette. The high school athletic team keeps alive the memory of the past with its name, the "Modeltowners."

The Gwinn Iron Ore District was on the easternmost portion of the Marquette Iron Range. Although Gwinn stands out as the foremost example of a model town in the area, it should not go unnoticed that the Marquette region had dozens of mines, mine locations and hundreds of company-built homes and even another model town at North Lake four miles west of Ishpeming. Another interesting development was the Ford purchase of two mines, the Blueberry near Ishpeming and the Imperial near Michigamme. The Imperial site developed into a model town, with home construction that included electrical power. These were mostly mining communities, but some took the next steps with furnaces producing pig iron or even forges to fabricate steel products. Neither was Marquette County void of lumber mills, with its company-owned homes. The Michigan Iron Industry Museum in Negaunee contains an excellent and wide variety of displays, artifacts and research materials related directly to the area's iron ore history. Marquette County hosts two major mining companies: Cliffs Natural Resources, which operates the Tilden and Empire Mines for iron ore, and Lundin Mining, which operates the Eagle Mine for nickel and copper.

KINGSFORD

The Iron Mountain community, near the southwestern border of Michigan with Wisconsin, was the recipient of major news in July 1920. The Ford Motor Company was going to open substantial facilities there for the construction of its automobiles, which utilized wood components in their auto bodies. The Iron Mountain area had been the focal point for iron ore mining activity along the Menominee Range. Area mines had been operational since the 1870s. With the iron mining activity on the decline, the community was delighted to have a new employer in its midst. There had been a great deal of speculation about the new facility's location, and the final location selected was an adjacent area to the west and south of the city of Iron Mountain. This four-and-a-half-square-mile area was situated between Iron Mountain and the Menominee River. It soon became the village of Kingsford, named after Edward Kingsford, who was married to Henry Ford's cousin. He owned and operated the Ford auto dealership in the region and provided much of the early local leadership for the venture. Initial buildings were to include a powerhouse, a sawmill and a body plant.

The undeveloped land area was purchased from the Iron Mountain Land and Mineral Company and soon bustled with activity. There was need to extend the Chicago, Milwaukee and St. Paul Railroad line to the industrial area, so six miles of track were laid. The name for the Ford operations became the Michigan Iron, Land and Lumber Company (sometimes abbreviated as MILLCO), later simply the Ford Motor Company; around town, it was referred to as the "Ford plant." Other early construction also included some boardinghouses (eventually eight, accommodating up to three hundred) and the first residential homes, called "the Ford addition." The homes contained six to eight rooms and initially were rented but later mostly were purchased by employees. In addition, there were many other privately owned residential areas or "subdivisions" developed throughout the community as the rapidly growing workforce overwhelmed the available housing. The modern bunkhouses were designed for single men and had two cots per room, electricity, steam heat and showers. One of the buildings functioned as a cafeteria for preparing and serving meals.

The magnitude of the development can be seen in the completion of the body plant, which occupied 125,000 square feet and used five hundred tons of steel. Eventually, there were three such facilities. At the same time, the number of kilns for drying the green lumber rose to fifty-two, and construction of a major hydroelectric facility was completed on the nearby Menominee River. The former power plant was converted for a foundry and blast furnace. A second lumber mill was added. Twenty-five filers were assigned the responsibility of keeping half a dozen varieties of saws and additional cutting devices sharpened. Lumber not otherwise utilized became shingles, laths or fuel. Seven large silos were constructed to store the charcoal production. Although the total Ford landholdings rose to 1 million acres, much timber was purchased from independent logging operators. One major Ford camp was located at Sidnaw, seventy miles to the north. By 1923, the body plant and sawmill were each running three shifts. The year before, the minimum wage had been established at six dollars per day. As the company scrambled to erect the needed buildings, employees had to be paid from an armored car. More houses were added in the Ford additions until the number rose to 160. These residential developments included water, gas, sewer, sidewalks, curbs and gutters, along with paved streets. Expansion activities occurred away from the industrial site, too. An office building was constructed, a commissary opened and a public recreational park developed.

The commissary was a large retail operation open to the general public. It included a variety of grocery items such as fresh produce and meat, as well as clothing and shoes. Purchases were on a cash basis. Apparently, the local retail establishments were not able to meet the demand from the dramatically increased population of the area. Other facilities that appeared on the scene included a clubhouse and a hospital. The clubhouse was basically a hotel and lounge facility for visiting Ford officials while in town. The first "hospital" resembled a modern clinic that was intended for the use of Ford employees who needed medical care. Before its opening, all employees and family members were charged $1.10 per month for access to one of the company-designated doctors in the area. (This was the same practice of the area's Oliver Mining Company.) That fee was eliminated with the opening of the hospital.

The shortage of housing continued to be a major priority for the community and Ford officials. The Ford addition homes were typically twenty-four by twenty-four or twenty-six by twenty-six. They were intentionally varied in design, one from another, if only in relatively minor features, such as having the living room and dining room positions interchanged from the right side of the house to the left. Some houses were a little larger for those in supervisory or managerial positions. Articles in the local newspaper touted "economy houses" that gave the highest-quality housing features for the lowest-possible cost for those who wanted to own their own homes outside the Ford additions. Other unique developments included the relocation of three homes from Calumet (130 miles to the north), where the copper mining activity was on the decline, and the practice of moving into a very small home with the goal of converting it into a garage at a later date. Whether one of the "Ford additions" or one of many privately funded subdivisions, road grading and developing the sites for water, sewer and electrical service was quite an endeavor for the small, newly developing community. Water was filtered at the Ford facilities (taken from the Menominee River), but the distribution system was installed and operated by the village.

The community around the Ford facility continued to grow until it was decided, in 1923, to establish a separate village of Kingsford from a portion of Breitung Township. Other signs of community growth included building three new schools in Breitung Township School District, road improvements and the village's first public safety officer, drugstore, bakery, grocery store and Lutheran church. By 1924, the population had soared to four thousand, and a community developed out of what had been vacant, undeveloped or farm land. The Iron Range Transportation Service provided bus service from the surrounding community to the mill. By 1925, the school population had doubled. The same year, a dance hall and theater opened. One unique form of entertainment was the showing of movies in a large tent. More conventional recreational activities included the formation of the Ford orchestra and a band. A Kingsford Community Club, which served as a professional club to "promote civic spirit," was formed to organize and stage a wide variety of social and cultural activities.

Company ownership and operation of housing and stores was not new for residents of the Iron Mountain community and Dickinson County. There were many such facilities throughout the community and neighboring areas. Local historian William Cummings has recorded company-owned houses and stores, such as those at the Pewabic and Chapin mines, where many in Iron Mountain worked. Immediately to the north, the Sagola Lumber Company had a boardinghouse and stores. To the southeast, in neighboring Vulcan, homes were owned by a mining company, as they also were in nearby Foster City, where the Morgan Lumber and Cedar Company operated a boardinghouse and a store. The Menominee Mining Company operated stores in nearby Waucedah, Vulcan and Norway.

In addition to the lumber production processes at the mill, there was the development of what was called the chemical plant. A highly modernized and automated facility was created that produced charcoal and wood alcohol and other byproducts from the drying, distilling and carbonizing stages. The facility became the largest of its type in the world, with most production utilized by Ford industries themselves. Later, "Kingsford charcoal" became a familiar name at many a backyard barbecue across the country. The chemical plant itself became dominant in the Ford complex, as it included two buildings six stories high. Equally impressive were the two 190-foot-high stacks from the site power plant. The auto body assembly included fifteen major steps that could be broken down into 420 separate operations as the methods of the Detroit assembly line were put into full practice. The number of employees at Kingsford continued to grow up to 7,500 in the 1920s, with a monthly payroll of $1 million. Although metal began replacing wood in the automobile frames, Kingsford's contribution expanded to include the exterior wood finish on the unique "woodie" station wagons in the Ford line. The Kingsford/Iron Mountain area's population reached a high of 18,000.

Operations at the Kingsford facility were greatly reduced after the United States' entry into World War II in December 1941. Reduced production of automobiles combined with outmigration to locations where employment opportunities were buoyed by wartime production. In 1942, Breitung schools reported a drop of two hundred children and loss of seventy families from the previous year. However, there was again good news when Ford got the contract for construction of wooden gliders at the Kingsford location. Two buildings idled from manufacturing station wagon bodies were quickly converted for assembling broad-winged invasion gliders that were critical to the European campaign. Although the primary materials for the glider did not come from the area forests, Kingsford's rail connections, labor force and facilities proved to be invaluable in its new role. The Kingsford facility received the prized "E" Award for the highest-quality war production from the U.S. Army-Navy department.

By 1951, the number of Ford employees at Kingsford had shrunk to 1,800, and the facilities were sold to a new entity called the Kingsford Corporation. Ownership of the new reduced facility consisted of officials from two area facilities, Lake Shore Engineering and Grede Foundries, along with major investors from Delaware. Ford donated 450 acres of land to what was now the city of Kingsford, Iron Mountain and Breitung Township for public recreational, civic and educational use. The land for a new hospital was donated to the county. Part of its legacy included having provided emergency fire services to the Kingsford community for twenty years, along with water purification services and an airport. (Community members were reminded in the newspaper to call the Ford Company if they wanted to report a fire.) By 1961, the Kingsford Company had closed its charcoal briquette production in Kingsford and laid off 354 employees. This marked the final chapter in the Ford story in Kingsford.

In 2015, Kingsford is a small, thriving community of five thousand. The region is home to a variety of small businesses and shops. These include Systems Control electronic equipment, Boss Snowplow, Verso Paper Corporation, Grede Foundry and Loadmaster refuse trucks and equipment. Together with neighboring Iron Mountain and Norway, they provide a strong commercial, industrial and educational base for the central Upper Peninsula. The area's history is well interpreted through three local museums: World War II Glider and Military Museum, Cornish Pumping Engine and Mining Museum and Menominee Range Historical Museum.

ALBERTA

Nine miles south of L'Anse and the Keweenaw Bay of Lake Superior lies Alberta, named for the daughter of Henry Ford's superintendent for Upper Peninsula operations. Founded in 1935, Alberta was to be Henry's response to the lack of visionary forest and business policies in the Upper Peninsula. The design of this model town was for its workers to divide their time between the lumber mill, logging in the forests and farming. Cutting of the trees would be selective, downing only the fully mature trees and leaving others for a later cut when they had developed. The long-term effects of the clear-cut practices in the timber industry were by then clearly evident, with large areas of the peninsula left in shambles. Homes for employees' families would not be rustic cottages but rather modern and attractive homes with the latest conveniences, such as running water and coal furnaces. The location of Alberta fit neatly near two other Ford facilities, L'Anse and Pequaming. Located on Lake Superior and directly north of Alberta, L'Anse was the shipping and departure point for the Ford lumber mills. Many of the employees who moved to Alberta were formerly Ford laborers at L'Anse, while many others commuted. Pequaming was a much older lumber mill and village that Henry Ford had purchased in 1923; it was also on the Lake Superior shore eight miles north of L'Anse. Alberta's assets as a location were its hardwood forests and a small stream that could be dammed to create a water reservoir needed for mill operations. Brian Cleven's master's thesis provides excellent historical detail of Ford's Alberta venture.

The preserved lumber mill at Alberta was smaller than most. *Photo by author.*

The town site was established in 1936 on a ten-acre site with large 90- by 150-foot lots. Twelve one-story houses were constructed, with no two of them alike. Each had seven to eight rooms and full basements. Exteriors

Alberta homes in 1939 or 1940, after the first families moved in 1937. *Michigan Tech Archives.*

were painted white, and interiors were varnished. Floors were made of maple; walls were plastered, insulated and heated with a coal furnace; and faucets provided hot water. Rent was twenty to twenty-five dollars per month. Estimates are that 12 to 15 percent of salaries were spent on housing rents. Original plans called for more homes, a park and playground, but they never materialized. Each home was inspected every six months to see if maintenance was needed.

Resembling as much a social experiment as an industrial venture, the plan was that workers would limit their time "on the clock" to four days and engage themselves in other activities such as farming for two days. The undertaking was consistent with the Ford program of establishing "village industries" across rural Michigan that operated somewhat as self-sufficient communities for farmers to enhance their incomes yet contributed to the overall Ford enterprise. The lumber mill itself was much smaller than the other facilities at L'Anse or Pequaming—a deliberate plan and something Henry Ford would have been fully cognizant of with his attention to detail. The plan stumbled from the beginning, as Ford operations began buying timber from independent suppliers rather than using their own extensive landholdings. At the same time, the soil in the area, while productive for trees, did not have similar value for other domestic growth. The length of the growing season did not work favorably, nor did the appetites of area deer. The number of employees at the mill remained in the low twenties. Alberta also did not develop the ancillary fixtures of a true community, such as retail, commercial and other services, such as a post office—all were lacking. Two schools were constructed, one for lower elementary and one for upper; high school students rode the Ford bus to Pequaming. The Alberta facility did attract many tourists and visitors to see a new approach for logging and a modern company town. Soon after World War II, all the Ford logging facilities had difficulty competing with private logging facilities. Priorities changed with new Ford leadership, and the ancillary ventures, such as lumber mills, were sold off. In 1954, the Alberta facility closed.

Later, in 1954, the facility and an adjacent 1,700-acre forest were donated to Michigan Technological University. It named it the Ford Center, and it became a combination museum, conference center and locale for conducting forestry-related research. It features a sawmill, a visitors' center, meeting rooms, dormitory facilities and town site buildings, some of which are available for vacation or long-term rental.

WHITE PINE

The unique story of White Pine is that the notable company town venture began so late in the history of the Upper Peninsula. It was 1951 when the go-ahead was given to resurrect the White Pine Mine, which had been purchased by the same Copper Range Company that had flourished in the Houghton region years earlier. This is not to say that the White Pine/Ontonagon area didn't have a long and interesting history that included logging, wood products manufacturing, silver mining and considerable copper mining. Although located on Lake Superior and having one of the largest rivers (the Ontonagon) in the Upper Peninsula, it tended to operate on the edges of the peninsula like its neighbors to the west (Ironwood) and to the north (Calumet/Hancock). It is flanked on its west by the Porcupine Mountains and to its south by a rugged, two-hundred-mile, sparsely populated expanse to Green Bay.

Chronologically, the Ontonagon area was home to some of the peninsula's first copper mining in the 1700s and later, just prior to the American Civil War. The famous discovery of the "Ontonagon Boulder" helped spark and fuel the "copper rush" to the northern peninsula. The huge copper mass (weighing between six and seven thousand pounds) was eventually transported to Detroit and, finally, to the Smithsonian museum in Washington, D.C. The copper mining industry in the Ontonagon region truly flourished (with more than one hundred sites explored or developed) until it was surpassed by that of the Calumet/Hancock/Houghton region after the Civil War. One such mine was the Minesota, notable for its sizeable production, medical services

At the Minesota Mine in the 1850s near Rockland, miners gathered for Contract Day, when teams of miners were paid for their production. *John M. Longyear Research Library.*

(first mining hospital) and unique spelling of its official name. Victoria operated as a company town, with medical services provided by medical school students, a moving picture theater and organized childcare. Early production from Ontonagon exceeded both its northern neighbor and any other region in the United States. However, yields gradually tapered off, and major regional employers became logging companies and the Diamond Match Company.

The area around White Pine, fifteen miles southwest of Ontonagon and adjacent to the Porcupine Mountains, was well known for copper-rich ore (located over what was known as the Nonesuch Lode). Just two miles away, the Nonesuch Mine had achieved an estimated accumulated yield of more than 180 tons of copper. Other than its unique name, the Nonesuch is recalled because an early owner had acquired it in exchange for a barrel of pork, a barrel of flour and some grocery items. The ore in this region was unique for two reasons: although there was some of the same native copper found in the Calumet/Houghton area, much appeared in a very fine form (called chalcocite or copper sulfide) and contained a relatively high level of silver. The regional folklore is filled with stories of mine employees who pocketed silver from the rock. Roy Hivala heard of one such man who accumulated enough to bankroll the purchase of new rifle.

After beginning in 1881, the White Pine ownership passed to the Calumet and Hecla Company of Calumet fame after 1910. Calumet and Hecla invested more than $2 million in exploration and development. It mined successfully for four years (especially during World War I), conducted exploratory diamond drilling and investigated new processes for recovering the fine particles of copper. After its accumulated production of 18 million pounds of copper fell off, it threw in the towel in 1929, and the mine was put on the auction block at a sheriff's auction in May, when it was sold for back taxes. Another amusing story is that the Copper Range bidder got quite a bargain, as the Calumet and Hecla representative had not been given authority to increase his bid by one dollar more than the level owed in taxes. With copper prices low, Copper Range focused on testing new processes to recover the small copper particles from the rock.

The time was right in the 1950s, as new technology had been developed for processing the copper from the White Pine and the United States' low copper reserves were considered a national defense liability, as the Korean War had begun and a long Cold War era was on the immediate horizon. The company received a loan of $67 million to develop copper mining facilities from the federal Defense Production Act. Copper Range pledged $13 million to this amount. Construction of the modern mine, mining facilities (such as a smelter) and town site began in 1952 and was completed in 1955. Just as mining and ore processing were increasingly sophisticated, complex and mechanized (including using hydraulics and diesel power), so was the town design, with a suburban/subdivision-type appearance to the residential areas and a shopping mall.

Copper Range constructed 150 homes for its new employees. In addition, dormitories for single men, apartments and a trailer park were provided. A dining hall was constructed for those without cooking facilities. Original plans called for twice the number of homes; however, it was soon discovered that employees in the 1950s were highly mobile and chose to drive from neighboring communities rather than relocate. A majority of the employees lived more than twenty-five miles from White Pine. Speculation was that given the roller-coaster nature of the mining industry, they were less inclined to pull up stakes from homes that they already owned. The majority of the commuters were from towns in Ontonagon County and neighboring Gogebic County, where iron mining had thrived years before. Private busses ran from Hurley Wisconsin near Ironwood, Iron River and Calumet to White Pine. Some existing housing dating back to the early 1900s was improved to accommodate more than one thousand construction workers. Copper Range employed a professional designer to ensure that new homes and residential areas looked up to 1950s cultural standards: streets were curved, garages were attached, lots were large and landscaping was completed. Streets were paved, and homes had in-floor heating to cope with severe winters. The sizes and presentation of the houses varied to avoid an appearance of repetition. Copper Range conducted maintenance on the rented homes but also encouraged owner purchase. A water supply line was run seven miles from Lake Superior, a phone system implemented and a sewer system installed. Arne Anderson did electrical work at the White Pine after his military discharge. He shared one of the company apartments with two other employees.

The town took on normal development. A volunteer fire department took shape, three churches were established, an elementary and high school were built and a twenty-bed hospital was completed. Schools and a hospital were built at company expense, although ongoing operation of the schools was the responsibility of the township board of education. The old system of charging White Pine employees fifty cents per month for medical care was brought into the twentieth century with membership in a medical insurance program. Other community hallmarks took shape, including a barbershop, an American Legion post and men's and women's clubs. Although the town did develop from the shell that was left from the World War I era, it didn't grow to the plans and satisfaction of Copper Range. The vast majority of employees chose to drive from their local communities rather than move to the "company town." Their ties to their own communities outweighed the time and danger of traveling long distances on highways to and from work. Company officials responded by encouraging the sale and financing of company houses and lots for private home construction. Likewise, they promoted establishment of a shopping mall with a modern grocery store, a drugstore and a bowling alley to improve the desirability of living in White Pine. One long-term employee, Albert Winberg of Kentwood, drove forty-seven miles one-way in all types of weather for the duration of the mine's operation. He worked on the mine's construction in sinking the shaft before it opened, at the mine as a section helper and at the copper refinery that operated after it closed. Common among many in the area, his father had worked at a sawmill while also farming.

At White Pine, major construction work and employment occurred above ground as well as below. *Michigan Tech Archives.*

The investment by the company and federal government flourished, with high production as the second-largest underground copper mine in the United States. However, Copper Range confronted other obstacles. In addition to competition from the large open-pit mines in the West (which were less expensive to operate than shaft facilities), its workforce was now unionized. Operations were plagued with prolonged contract negotiations and strikes that negatively affected the supply of labor, both in quantity and quality. Many skilled laborers moved out of the area while laid off or during a strike. This was also a time of ever-increasing environmental regulations to which they had to adapt in their operations. The drop in copper prices in the mid-'70s was the beginning of the end. Production was reduced at the mine, and this led to layoffs. Copper Range attempted sales to Louisiana Land & Exploration and Echo Bay of Canada. A twenty-one-month strike led by the United Steelworkers was ended by an Employee Stock Ownership Plan and then a later sale, this time to a Canadian firm, Metall Mining.

Attempts by Copper Range to resurrect the mine were stalled by environmental issues and, finally, by lack of capital. Some small businesses were able to utilize some of the closed facilities for a limited time, but White Pine's days as an industrial center appeared over. During the twenty years of decline from 1975 to 1995, businesses were closed, school enrollment dwindled, the hospital was downgraded to a medical clinic, homes were sold and, finally, the high school was closed. The rise and fall of the Michigan copper industry and company towns was broadly represented at White Pine.

The White Pine site in 2014 operated as an industrial park for small businesses and a power plant. The most interesting development has been SubTerra's underground growth business for pharmaceuticals in empty mine shafts. Recent closures of the copper refinery in White Pine and the paper mill in Ontonagon have put more pressure on the local economy, which is tied to forestry, small manufacturing shops, tourism and recreation, especially with the nearby Porcupine Mountains Wilderness State Park. The Canadian Highland Copper Company has recently purchased the White Pine facility from Copper Range and is doing exploratory drilling. Hopes are high in the community for a reopened White Pine mine.

EPILOGUE

What conclusions can be reached about company towns in the Upper Peninsula? Were they simply an economic model that was relevant for a period of time but passed out of fashion? Was the economic model incompatible with trade unionism, the Progressive era and the emerging American values of homeownership and economic independence? Were they an example of immigrants being exploited by American capitalists? Were they a function of the natural resource–based economy of the region that was destined to expire? Were they a bona fide response to a needed labor force that had insufficient resources for homeownership? Alison Hoagland has suggested that the relationship between company and employee resembled a type of negotiation where both sides recognized that company housing was a bargain for both sides. Andrea Tone noted that companies preferred corporate-based benefits to government-sponsored programs. Were they an example of the adage that power corrupts and absolute power corrupts absolutely? Are company towns an example of how far employers will maximize their influence over employees and communities when allowed? Or are they an example of how employees and corporations can, over time, find some common ground? The simple existence of company towns in isolated, resource-rich areas in the twenty-first century and unique pockets of the high-tech industry suggests that there is still relevance today—likewise for the issue of the role or limits of industry's role in provision of social welfare, from health insurance to retirement programs. Are these benefits the responsibility of the employer, the government or the individual?

The first thing that struck me with the "passing" of the company towns was that it does not appear the host industries failed or passed out of existence because of the company town model. They passed because their supply of timber or minerals ran low or because the processing technology changed to limit their relevance. Neither did they normally pass because their offerings of pay, medical coverage and housing were insufficient. Certainly, when the communities' unemployment rates rose, employees left, and yes, the copper mines and Wisconsin Land and Lumber had labor shortages, and these do appear to have been a result of noncompetitive rates of pay. After watching his own father's struggle in the Keweenaw copper mines, Dale Julien's father left for the Ford plant in Detroit. However, these were hardly a rejection of the company town model but rather of job instability and noncompetitive rates of pay. Still, I was surprised at the level of what appeared to be employee satisfaction from Bay de Noc to the Keweenaw. Perhaps this is a case of a bad job being better than no job at all. Even so, there were many examples of employee appreciation for the company and its services in the community. Certainly, they were not universal, with notable examples at Hermansville and with the Keweenaw copper strike.

Another issue of interest was the degree of corporate influence exercised by the industries. Clearly they were very active in discouraging and preventing bona fide unionization at their facilities through the use of spies and informants. Only Copper Range at White Pine had a unionized workforce during most of its tenure. Favoritism in treatment of employees extended beyond the workplace and into the community when decisions on housing were being made. In some cases, the security detail of the company was the local community law enforcement agency. This extended to strong company representation on township, school and county boards. Company interests were in keeping taxes low and ensuring that their priorities for services were met. Reports indicate that company methods for accomplishing such were heavy-handed to say the least. In Canada, a law had to be passed to ensure that communities had civil authorities beyond those of the company.

Company ownership of houses was an appropriate solution on several counts. Immigrants arriving from Europe had frequently exhausted their resources on the ocean trip over, so there were no funds for land or home purchase. As their first place of employment and residence, many weren't ready to "put down roots." Some did not intend to stay here and came with the intention of earning some cash and returning to the homeland. Frequently, all land near the mine was owned by the company, and in the days before the automobile, transportation to and from the workplace would have been an issue. By all appearances, rents were low and not a major company revenue stream, so the companies were not gouging employees. Rents were normally a relatively minor percentage of workers' income.

Many of the same issues apply to the company stores. At many locations, there were no other options for retail trade or those that did exist were at too great a distance where transportation options were few. The life cycle for many mines was short, so why would anyone want to invest in establishing a store when the future looked so unpredictable? Profits from the stores do not appear to have been a major revenue stream for the companies either; rather, their interest was to keep prices low so the employees could tolerate low wages. Clearly, today's perspective is that they stepped over the line in restricting the sale of alcohol in those stores, yet we are comfortable with the contemporary government restricting the sale of tobacco and marijuana.

Were there abuses by company officials with respect to taking unfair advantage due to their influence? I am sure there were. Was it much beyond what normally occurs by businesses or society, either then or today? In general, I doubt it. Based on conversations I've had with those who worked in such towns or other indicators, like the post-strike hearings of life in the Copper County, employees were not that dissatisfied with the company paternalism. Basic rate of pay was a higher issue. Yes, owners and investors made money to a degree that many would see as inappropriate compared to what industry laborers made. Is it more out of balance than such today? I doubt it. Others might well argue otherwise—that the risk of the investors or owners was due a generous reward. Were company towns in Michigan's Upper Peninsula an anomaly, social injustice or merely part of the texture of the emerging past? I suspect the reader can find fodder for either or other interpretations, depending on the perspective he or she brings to the question.

How great a theme is the company town in Upper Peninsula history? How does it compare with investors from Boston, New York or Chicago making the local business decisions? Can it compare with the impact of the 1842 treaty with the Chippewa, the railroads and construction of the locks at Sault Ste. Marie? I can't help but wonder if the model somehow didn't help frame notions in unions of what benefits an employer should provide, such as medical services or pensions. Fortunately, we have concrete reminders, such as the Fayette town site, to prompt our thoughts about change and the respective roles of corporate and private citizens. Hopefully this work will encourage the reader to investigate a community further through one of the books listed in the bibliography or a visit to an Upper Peninsula community itself.

BIBLIOGRAPHY

Alanen, Arnold R. "Gwinn: A Model Town 'Without Equal.'" *Michigan History Magazine* (November/December 1994): 33–35.

———. "Homes on the Range: Settling the Penokee-Gogebic Iron Ore District of Northern Wisconsin and Michigan." *Wisconsin Land and Life*. Edited by R. Ostergren and T. Vale. Madison: University of Wisconsin Press, 1997.

———. *The Settlements of Marquette County, Michigan*. Negaunee, MI: Economic Development Corporation of the County of Marquette, 1991.

Boyum, Burton H. *The Saga of Iron Mining in Michigan's Upper Peninsula*. Marquette, MI: John M. Longyear Library, 1977.

Boyum, Burton, Will Brideson and Thomas Pellow. "History of Iron Ore Mining." *Diamond Jubilee: 75th Anniversary of the Founding of the Village of Gwinn and Gwinn High School, June 25–July 4, 1983*. Gwinn, MI. Jubilee Committee, 1983.

Brayak, Jean Peterson. *The Story of Ford River Township*. Escanaba, MI: Photo Offset Press, 1973.

Case, Charles M. *Hermansville from the Beginning*. Hermansville, MI: IXL Museum, 2001.

Chabot, Chris. *Tales of White Pine*. Ontonagon, MI: Ontonagon Herald, 1979.

Chaput, Donald. *The Cliff: America's First Great Copper Mine*. Kalamazoo, MI: Sequoia Press, 1971.

Cleven, Brian E. "Henry Ford's 'Tasty Little Town.'" *Michigan History Magazine* (January/February 1999): 18–23.

———. "Pequaming and Alberta: Henry Ford's Model Towns." Master's thesis. Michigan Technological University, 1997.

Cummings, William John, ed. *Kingsford: The Town Ford Built in Dickinson County, Michigan*. Kingsford, MI: C.J. Graphics, 1998.

Dodge, Roy L. *Michigan Ghost Towns of the Upper Peninsula*. Holt, MI: Thunder Bay Press, 2007.

Doyle, Earl L., and Ruth B. MacFarlane. *The History of Pequaming*. Hancock, MI: Book Concern Printers, 2002.

Dreier, Edward. *The Story of Blaney Park*. N.p., n.d.

Fayette Historic Townsite. 3rd ed. Lansing: Michigan History Magazine, 2014.

Fields, Richard A. *Range of Opportunity: A Historic Study of the Copper Range Company*. Hancock, MI: Quincy Mine Hoist Association, 1997.

Friggens, Thomas. "Fayette: 1867–1891 Economic and Cultural Origins, Development and Decline of a Michigan Town." Master's thesis. Wayne State University, 1973.

Gates, William B. *Michigan Copper and Boston Dollars: An Economic History of the Michigan Copper Mining Industry*. New York: Russell & Russell, 1951.

Hiawatha National Forest Oral History Series Transcripts. La Crosse, WI: U.S. West Research Inc., n.d.

Hoagland, Alison K. *Mine Towns: Buildings for Workers in Michigan's Copper Country*. Minneapolis: University of Minnesota Press, 2010.

Hollingsworth, Sandra. *The Atlantic: Copper and Community South of Portage Lake*. Hancock, MI: John H. Foster Press, 1978.

Huttenstine, Jan. *Remotely Yours*. Paradise, MI: East West Press, 2010.

IXL Museum. *Hermansville, Michigan, the People and Their Legacy*. Hermansville, MI: Bresnan Communications, n.d.

Jacques, Thomas Edward. *A History of the Garden Peninsula*. Iron Mountain, MI: Mid-Peninsula Library Cooperative, 1979.

Jamison, James K. *The Mining Ventures of this Ontonagon Country*. Ontonagon, MI: self-published, 1950.

Jobst, Jack. "A Resort Called Blaney." *Michigan History Magazine* (July/August 2008): 42–49.

Karamanski, Theodore. *Deep Woods Frontier: A History of Logging in Northern Michigan*. Detroit: Wayne State University Press, 1989.

Kolehmainen, John. *The Finns in America: A Students' Guide to Localized History*. New York: Teachers College Press, 1968.

Lamberg, Glenn. *Nahma Interviews*. Nahma, MI: Nahma Township Historical Society, 2013–14.

Lankton, Larry. *Hollowed Ground: Copper Mining and Community Building on Lake Superior, 1840s–1990s.* Detroit: Wayne State University, 2010.

Lombard, Frances Maas. *Shavings and Sawdust.* N.p., 1993.

Magnaghi, Russell M. *The Way It Happened: Settling Michigan's Upper Peninsula.* Iron Mountain, MI: Mid-Peninsula Library Cooperative, 1982.

Martin, Jack. *Memories of Early Gwinn.* N.p., 1995.

Michigan Karst Conservatory. Caves.org/conservancy/mkc.

Moreau, Clarence. *The Story of Simmon's Wood.* Hermansville, MI: IXL Museum, n.d.

Moreau, Clarence, and the Newton Township Historical Society. *Simmons Memories.* Gould City, MI: Newton Township Historical Society, 2014.

Reynolds, Terry S. "We Were Satisfied with It." *Michigan History Magazine* (November/December 1994): 24–32.

Stevens, Deidre. "Blaney Park's Birdman." *Michigan History Magazine* (July/August 2008): 51–53.

Taylor, Sprague. *Tahquamenon Country: A Look at Its Past.* East Lansing: Michigan State University Press, 2008.

Thurner, Arthur W. *Strangers and Sojourners: A History of Michigan's Keweenaw Peninsula.* Detroit: Wayne State University Press, 1994.

Wakefield, Larry. *Ghost Towns of Michigan.* Vol. 2. Holt, MI: Thunder Bay Press, 1995.

White Pine Lake Copper. New York: Copper Range Company, 1962.

White Pine Story. White Pine, MI: White Pine Copper Company, 1967.

Whitney, Mark. *Fiborn Quarry: Then and Now.* Ann Arbor: Michigan Karst Conservancy, 2014.

Worth, Jean. "A History of Hermansville." Unpublished manuscript, August 2014.

NEWSPAPERS

Daily Tribune-Gazette.

Escanaba Daily Press.

Evening News.

Iron Mountain Press.

St. Ignace News.

INDEX

N

O

P

Q

S

V

W

ABOUT THE AUTHOR

A former resident of Alpena and Detroit, Christian Holmes has lived in Escanaba, Michigan, since 1976. He graduated from Wayne State University, where he obtained degrees in English composition, philosophy and library science. A passion for research, writing and the history of Michigan led to his interest in company towns in the Upper Peninsula.